LAILA HELMY

DUBAI

TRAVEL GUIDE

A UNIQUE
Dubai Travel Guide
WITH
55
UNFORGETTABLE
Experiences

CONTENTS

Deira

Jebel Ali

Dubai Surroundings

Emergency

Fire Department: Tel. 9 97

Ambulance: Tel. 9 98

Police: Tel. 9 99

OVERVIEW

Our 55 experiences in Dubai are color-coded by region. Within each region, the experiences are organized by their approximate duration (2 hours, 4 hours, and 8 hours).

4
3
1
6
2
5

INTRODUCTION

The Burj Khalifa

Experience Dubai, where modern skyscrapers blend seamlessly with a desert backdrop reminiscent of 1001 Arabian Nights. Dubai, the epicenter of the United Arab Emirates, awaits you with an extraordinary mix of culture, innovation, and luxury.

Imagine standing on the shores of the Persian Gulf, admiring the impressive skyline of Dubai. Glittering skyscrapers soar into the sky, as if they were a modern tribute to the cityscape. The Burj Khalifa, the tallest building in the world, rises majestically, inviting you to view the city from a bird's-eye perspective. Dubai is the result of human creativity and visionary dreams. Where else can you lounge on the beach in the morning, swim with sharks in the afternoon, race down ski slopes, enjoy a desert sunset from the world's highest observation deck in the evening, and spend your nights in a Bedouin camp? This variety of activities is unique in the world, making Dubai a truly special travel destination.

While experiencing Dubai's astonishing modernity, be sure to take time to explore the old souks. Souks are traditional markets that immerse you in Dubai's historic culture. Step into the famous Gold Souk, where the shimmering metal gleams in all its glory. Or indulge your senses at the

Spice Souk, with its exotic aromas, and get to know authentic Arabic culture up close.

But Dubai is not just a place where the past meets the present; it is also a canvas for the future. Artificial palm islands and floating luxury resorts above crystal-clear waters showcase cutting-edge engineering. Adventure seekers will find a true paradise in Dubai with desert safaris, water sports, and thrilling theme parks.

Dubai's culinary scene is as diverse as its people. Savor the flavors of traditional Arabic cuisine or indulge in international gourmet experiences - Dubai offers a truly global feast for the senses.

Dubai is a city where dreams come true and expectations are surpassed. It invites you on a journey that will expand your horizons, spark your imagination, and enchant your senses.

The famous luxury hotel Burj Al Arab

EXCITING FACTS

Dubai has a population of around 3.5 million. The average age is about 30 years, and among the residents, there are 15 billionaires (with numbers on the rise).

Arabic is the official language spoken in Dubai, **but you can easily communicate in English almost everywhere.**

The UAE Dirham (abbreviation AED), often referred to simply as Dirham, is the currency of the United Arab Emirates.

Upon your arrival at Dubai Airport, **you will receive a free visa that is valid for 30 days.** It is important to note that your passport must have a minimum validity of six months.

Dubai has two airports: Dubai International Airport (DXB) and Al Maktoum International Airport (DWC). Dubai International Airport is the largest and most well-known airport in Dubai. Al Maktoum International Airport is located near the Jebel Ali area.

The time difference in Dubai is +4 hours (during daylight saving time, it's only +3 hours).

The best time to visit Dubai is from November to March. During this period, the temperatures are cooler, ranging from about 24 to 31 degrees Celcius. From April to October, temperatures can rise above 40 degrees Celcius.

Since 2022, weekends in Dubai last 2.5 days, from Friday afternoon to Sunday. Prior to this, Friday and Saturday were considered the weekend. From 1971 to 1999, only Friday was recognized as the "weekend". However, the new 2.5-day rule does not apply to the construction and hospitality industries, where workers often have 6- or even 7-day work weeks.

Around 20 to 25 years ago, Dubai was mostly an empty desert, but the city has developed tremendously thanks to the vision of its rulers.

At 828 meters, the Burj Khalifa is the tallest building in the world, while Dubai continues to build new skyscrapers.

Over 85% of Dubai's population are foreigners.

Public displays of affection, such as kissing and hugging, are not allowed. In the worst case, you could end up in jail for it.

Dubai offers pink taxis with female drivers to accommodate women who feel uncomfortable riding with male drivers.

For a long time, there were no income taxes in Dubai, making it very attractive for expats. However, a new tax law is set to change that.

Palm Jumeirah is one of the boldest construction projects in the world. **An astonishing 10 million truckloads of sand were needed to create the artificial palm-shaped island,** which can even be seen from space.

The Burj Al Arab calls itself the "first 7-star hotel" in the world. The interiors of the hotel are gilded with an incredible 1,790 square meters of 24-carat gold. Room rates can reach up to around £17,000 per night.

Dubai came up with a radical idea for people looking to shed a few extra pounds. **The government announced that for every 2 kg of weight lost, they would offer 2 grams of gold.** They truly took the motto "Every calorie counts" seriously.

Dubai strives to be number one in everything and has set countless world records. **One of them was having the longest driverless metro until 2009.** Now, Singapore holds the record for the most extensive driverless public transit system.

Alcohol consumption in Dubai is regulated and only allowed for those aged 21 and older. Additionally, dancing in public is also prohibited.

Female tourists are not required to wear a veil, but there are certain rules regarding clothing. **Women should avoid overly revealing outfits and cover more skin than they show, while men should also dress appropriately.** However, theory and practice can differ in Dubai. Nowadays, many freedoms are tolerated, but it's still important to dress respectfully and appropriately.

The police in Dubai use luxury cars such as **Lamborghini Aventador, Ferraris, Bugattis, and Aston Martins.**

In addition to regular ATMs, Dubai also has gold ATMs, the city plays a significant role in the global gold trade.

Eating and drinking are prohibited in the Dubai Metro.

Despite people from all over the world living in Dubai, the city's crime rate remains at 0%. This may be due to the high level of surveillance and police presence, combined with very strict penalties and a lack of human rights laws in the country.

At camel races, **remote-controlled robots are used as jockeys instead of humans.**

"The Tower" is an observation tower currently under construction in Dubai. **Its estimated height is expected to be between 928 and 1,400 meters, which will surpass the Burj Khalifa as the tallest building.**

The water consumption in the UAE is the highest in the world due to the heat and air conditioning.

Believe it or not, less than a decade ago, Dubai had no address system – meaning no street or building numbers. Every package or envelope contained carefully written instructions on where it needed to go.

On average, it rains only 25 days a year in Dubai, with February being the most prone to rain.

The UAE has strict limitations on freedom of speech. **It is prohibited to criticize the government, the police, or the royal families in any way.** People have been imprisoned for posting satirical videos and tweets about the government.

Homosexuality is illegal in the UAE, with penalties of up to 10 years in prison. LGBTQ+ travelers should be mindful of their surroundings, remain discreet, and prioritize their safety to ensure an enjoyable trip.

The holy month of Ramadan is the 9th month of the Islamic lunar calendar and starts on a different date each year. However, Ramadan typically takes place early in the year (between February and April) and lasts about 30 days. **Devout Muslims observe introspection, reflection, and abstinence during Ramadan. In public, it is prohibited to eat, drink, or smoke during the day throughout Ramadan in Dubai, even for non-Muslims and tourists.** After sunset, Dubai comes alive as eating and drinking are permitted during the night.

HISTORY

The wisdom of Dubai's rulers has shown that a simple fishing village can grow into a thriving metropolis. This story, anchored in the heart of trade routes, is divided into two distinct eras: before and after the discovery of precious oil.

In the 19th century, Dubai was still a simple village on the shores of a creek. However, due to its strategically advantageous location, the Dubai Creek (an inlet of the Persian Gulf) quickly transformed into a thriving center for fishing and pearl trading. The market on the Deira side of the creek gained fame throughout the Middle East. The Al Maktoum dynasty played a crucial role in this development, even signing an agreement with the British government, placing Dubai under British protection.

The pearl industry reached its peak until the emergence of artificial pearls revolutionized the market and challenged Dubai's economy. After the decline of the pearl trade, the city had to rethink its strategy.

At that time, the United Arab Emirates did not yet exist in its current form. There were seven emirates, including the well-known Abu Dhabi, Sharjah, and Dubai. A border conflict between Dubai and Abu Dhabi even led to armed confrontations. The history of Dubai after the discovery of oil in the 20th century unfolded at a rapid pace. British troops withdrew, allowing Dubai to stand on its own. During the reign of Sheikh Rashid, the decision was made to form the United Arab Emirates (UAE). In the early 1970s, the seven emirates united to form the UAE. Dubai and Abu Dhabi joined under the condition that they would retain control over the government and hold veto power on matters of national security.

Although Abu Dhabi serves as the capital of the UAE, Dubai remains a key hub for both economics and politics. The city has significantly contributed to the development of culture and architecture.

The discovery of oil led to investments in public infrastructure. Numerous schools, hospitals, roads, and buildings were constructed. Sheikh Zayed Road, now lined with futuristic skyscrapers and modern infrastructure, was once surrounded by desert.

However, the city also experienced challenging times, such as the Persian Gulf War of 1990, in which the UAE participated as military supporters. This had a negative impact on the country's economy. Nevertheless, Dubai managed to recover from the economic downturn and offset its losses.

In the 1990s, Dubai decided to invest in infrastructure and position itself as a major tourism destination – a necessity given its limited oil resources. This opened up alternative revenue streams to ensure sustainable development. Building a metropolis from scratch was a monumental challenge, especially with global competition among travel destinations. However, Dubai's business model faced this challenge with determination.

Today, Dubai has become a hub for tourism, trade, and entertainment. With a high quality of life, world-class hotels, and numerous skyscrapers, the city attracts millions of visitors. As a result, Dubai has emerged as one of the most visited cities in the world.

FOR SAVERS

Traditional Abras

Outside of Dubai's peak season from November to March, the summer months offer great opportunities for budget travelers.

Hotels provide attractive deals, flight prices drop, and top shopping malls entice visitors with discounts. Thanks to air-conditioned indoor locations, you can manage the summer heat and still explore the city. During the off-season, luxury beach resorts also offer more affordable rates.

Travel economically with the Dubai Metro, which covers key areas such as the airport and popular tourist spots. Most major shopping centers, like Mall of the Emirates or Dubai Mall, are connected to the metro network. With a Nol card, you can access Dubai's public transportation system. The cards can be purchased and topped up at metro and bus stations, as well as in various malls and supermarkets (more details can be found in the next chapter "The Nol Cards").

For a charming ride across the Creek, hop on traditional water taxis known as Abras. These wooden boats take you to the other side of the city for a small fare, offering picturesque views of traditional Arabian houses, wind towers, and minarets, set against the backdrop of the modern skyline.

In addition to luxury resorts and hotels, you'll also find more affordable options in Dubai. Keep an eye out for Airbnb listings or hotel apartments in central locations. Apartments and villas often come with fully equipped kitchens, allowing you to cook and save on meal costs. Alternatively, opt for a budget-friendly hotel outside the city center that's connected to the metro. Fortunately, Dubai offers many budget hotels with convenient access to the city's top attractions.

In the neighborhoods of Al Karama, Bur Dubai, and Deira, you'll find small cafés and restaurants offering delicious dishes at affordable prices. Highly recommended are the Pakistani dishes at "Ravi's" or the Iranian kebabs at "Al Ustad Special Kebab". You can also find budget-friendly fast food options and snacks in the food courts of shopping malls.

Plan your trip with the Dubai Pass and enjoy discounted access to some of the city's top attractions, tours, and sightseeing packages. Depending on the duration and option, prices for the Dubai Pass start at around £125 for 7 days (more information available at www.iventurecard.com/ae/dubai-pass/).

Many places in Dubai also offer free access to attractions or alternative viewpoints. For example, free public beaches often provide just as stunning views and perfect access to the sea. Visit Kite Beach to sunbathe, swim in the sea, or play volleyball – all for free. You can also experience the free Dubai Fountain sound and light show, set against the backdrop of the world's tallest tower, the Burj Khalifa. For a leisurely waterfront stroll with stunning city views, visit the Viewing Point in Dubai Creek Harbour or the Dubai Marina Walk.

Dubai Metro

THE NOL-CARDS

The Nol cards in Dubai function as contactless payment methods for the city's public transportation system. These cards allow passengers to conveniently and cashlessly pay for rides on various modes of transport, including the Dubai Metro, buses, trams, and water buses.

The card operates on a prepaid system, meaning users need to load money onto the card in advance to pay for their rides. Nol cards can be purchased at Nol machines at stations, stops, and other points of sale. Alternatively, they can also be registered and ordered online through the Roads & Transport Authority (RTA) website in Dubai.

Let's take a closer look at the different types of Dubai Nol cards. Prices vary depending on the card chosen. The Silver Nol card is ideal for regular travelers. This card offers unlimited access to all RTA transportation options in Dubai and has one of the highest reload limits (up to approximately £1,000).

The Gold Nol card is essentially the same as the Silver card but grants access to the Gold Class on all RTA transportation. Gold Class carriages are for those who prefer to travel in first class. Every Dubai Metro train has a Gold Class carriage, offering larger, more comfortable seats with extra legroom. Gold Class carriages are usually less crowded than standard carriages.

The Personal Nol card in Dubai is one of the most common options. Not only does it allow you to recover your balance in case of loss or theft, but it also provides discounts on fares.

The Dubai Metro Red Card is ideal for tourists visiting the city. This temporary card is perfect for visitors staying longer than 3 days and planning to use public transportation. The card is valid for metro, buses, and trams, but not for ferries, Abras, or taxis. For more information on the different cards, you can visit www.rta.ae.

FOOD & DRINK

Arabic coffee

Dubai is not only known for its towering skyscrapers and extravagant shopping experiences but also for its rich and diverse culinary scene.

The city offers a wide range of restaurants, cafés, and street food stalls, all serving an array of flavors and delightful experiences. Whether you have a taste for traditional Arabic cuisine or crave international gourmet delicacies, Dubai has something to satisfy every palate.

Among the beverages, Arabic coffee is particularly popular in Dubai. Prepared from freshly ground coffee beans, Arabic coffee boasts a unique flavor and intense aroma. It is often served in small cups and symbolizes hospitality.

In addition to coffee, tea is one of the most common beverages in the UAE. "Karak Chai" is a particularly popular tea, prepared with spices like cardamom and cinnamon. It is often served with sweetened condensed milk and has a strong, spicy flavor. Among refreshing drinks, "Jellab" is very popular. Made from date syrup, grape syrup, and rose syrup, it is often served with ice and nuts. It has a sweet and fruity note, making it ideal for hot days. The drink "Laban" is also very refreshing; however, it is a yogurt-based drink. Slightly tangy in taste, it is often enjoyed as a thirst quencher.

When visiting Dubai, it's highly recommended to try the exquisite Arabic cuisine. Sample the traditional Mezze (the word "Mezze" comes from the Arabic verb "Mazmaza", meaning "to nibble"), which consists of appetizers like hummus, tabbouleh, falafel, and freshly baked bread. Among the traditional bread varieties, "Khobz Al Khameer" is noteworthy – a soft, slightly sweet yeast flatbread. Also popular is "Rigag", a thin and crispy bread that can be topped with either savory or sweet ingredients. Emirati pancakes known as "Chebab" are another specialty, often served for breakfast.

Traditional mezze

A very traditional dish is "Al Harees", made from wheat semolina, meat, and spices. It is slow-cooked until it reaches a creamy consistency. Another popular dish is "Machboos", a savory rice dish with various meats and spices, often garnished with roasted nuts and raisins.

For a unique experience, you can try a "Camel Burger", made from camel meat, which actually tastes quite similar to a beef burger. Also worth mentioning is "Ghuzi", a hearty dish featuring roasted lamb or goat served over spiced rice, often prepared for special occasions.

Be sure to save some room for dessert. Dubai is known for its exquisite and extravagant sweets. "Luqaimat", also called "Lokma", is a very popular Arabic dessert made from small, crispy dough balls dipped in sugar syrup. Or try the sweet "Baklava", which consists of layers of thin pastry filled with nuts and soaked in syrup.

Machboos

In addition to traditional and classic desserts, it's well worth trying the local dates. Dates in Dubai have a distinctive and delicious taste, often described as sweet, juicy, and slightly sticky. The Middle East is renowned for its high-quality dates, and Dubai offers a wide variety of types, each with unique flavors and textures.

Alongside authentic Arabic cuisine, Dubai is also known for its diverse food culture, beautifully reflecting the city's multiculturalism. Visitors can enjoy a range of international delights, from spicy Indian dishes to the finest Japanese sushi and Italian pasta. The possibilities are truly endless.

These diverse foods and beverages provide a glimpse into the rich Emirati cuisine and the flavors of the region. In Dubai, you'll find a vast selection of restaurants and street vendors offering these culinary delights.

SHOPPING

Dubai is known worldwide as a shopping paradise, offering an almost endless selection of shopping options for every taste and budget. From modern malls featuring international luxury brands to traditional bazaars, you'll find everything your shopping heart desires here.

Dubai's shopping malls are not just places to shop, but also architectural masterpieces and entertainment hubs. The Dubai Mall, the largest shopping center in the world, houses hundreds of stores, including international luxury brands like Gucci, Chanel, and Louis Vuitton. At the Mall of the Emirates, you can not only shop but also visit Ski Dubai, an indoor ski resort in the middle of the desert. The Ibn Battuta Mall, named after the famous Arab explorer's journeys, features various themed sections that reflect the countries he visited.

If you're looking for traditional souvenirs, be sure to visit the charming souks. The Gold Souk is famous for its impressive selection of gold and diamond jewelry, while the Spice Souk overwhelms the senses with exotic aromas. In numerous smaller markets, you'll find not only spices but also intricately handcrafted carpets, authentic textiles, and souvenirs.

For modern shopping and an inspiring experience, visit the Dubai Design District (d3), where you'll find stylish boutiques offering local designer goods, trendy accessories, and unique artworks. Alternatively, explore the open-air "City Walk" shopping center, a blend of shopping and entertainment where luxury and creativity go hand in hand.

Tucked away from the well-known malls and markets is the Al Fahidi Souk, also known as Meena Bazaar, in the Bur Dubai district, offering an authentic and charming shopping experience. This market is less crowded than some of the more famous shopping destinations, allowing you to stroll leisurely through the stalls. Here, you'll find clothing from regional artists, perfumes, antiques, cosmetics, and much more.

Most shops are open seven days a week. In traditional markets and souks, haggling is customary. Prices usually start about 25% higher than their actual value, and you can be bold by making an offer first. When bargaining in Dubai's souks, it's important to show interest, remain friendly, and propose a reasonable price. Be patient, explore alternatives, and know when to stop. Respect the local culture and enjoy the experience of negotiating.

Whether you're looking for luxury items, traditional craftsmanship, or modern trends, Dubai offers a shopping experience like no other.

Spice Souk

55 EXPERIENCES MAP

In the following section of our travel guide, we present our 55 exciting experiences and activities in Dubai.

To help you plan your trip optimally, you will have free access to our "Google MyMaps" map of Dubai. On this online map, you will find all 55 experiences precisely marked, giving you a perfect overview of Dubai in connection with our activities and attractions.

Simply scan the QR code below or access the online map directly via the provided link: **www.gamikaze.ch/maps/dubai-en**

METRO MAP

Access the Dubai Metro map quickly and easily online, or print the map for your convenience.

Simply scan the QR code below or access the Metro map directly via the provided link: **www.gamikaze.ch/maps/dubai-en/metro**

#1

2h

BURJ KHALIFA

Spectacular Views from the Tallest Building in the World

In Dubai, everything is bigger, more beautiful, or taller than in other cities around the world. This principle is especially evident in the city's monumental landmark – the Burj Khalifa. Towering at an astonishing height of 828 meters, the skyscraper dwarfs all other buildings in the emirate. Since its completion in April 2008, it has proudly stood as the tallest structure in the world.

A significant moment in the history of the Burj Khalifa was its grand inauguration on January 4, 2010, when the world's tallest structure changed its name from "Burj Dubai" to "Burj Khalifa". The new name honors the former President of the United Arab Emirates, Khalifa bin Zayed Al Nahyan, who generously supported the project.

With 189 floors, the Burj Khalifa is not only the tallest building but also offers unique experiences. A major part of the film "Mission Impossible - Ghost Protocol", starring Tom Cruise, was actually shot in the Burj Khalifa. The upper floors are home to luxury apartments, elegant offices, and exquisite restaurants, including the world's first Armani Hotel, personally curated by the renowned Italian fashion designer Giorgio Armani.

For visitors, the Burj Khalifa offers unforgettable observation decks with

Burj Khalifa at Sunset

View from the Burj Khalifa

Staircase in the Burj Khalifa

Burj Khalifa Entrance

stunning views of Dubai's skyline. Particularly impressive is the 360-degree observation deck on floors 124 and 125 ("At the Top"), where you can enjoy a spectacular panoramic view of the city. Even higher, on the 148th floor at 555 meters, there is another viewing platform ("At the Top SKY"), offering visitors a nearly dizzying perspective. However, the "At the Top SKY" platform does not provide a full 360-degree view and is significantly less crowded than the 124th and 125th floors.

The experience at the Burj Khalifa is enriched by details like the two gold ATMs, which have been in the building since February 2011. Here, visitors can purchase not banknotes but precious gold bars weighing up to one ounce – a unique souvenir of this extraordinary experience.

The early evening hours are particularly popular, as the sunset bathes the city in a soft glow, and the view from above is simply breathtaking (ticket prices during sunset hours are accordingly a bit higher). For a more intimate experience, we recommend visiting late in the evening or at night, when there are fewer visitors, allowing you to quietly enjoy Dubai's illuminated skyline.

Tickets for the Burj Khalifa are available both on-site and online. Various ticket options are available, including combo tickets that also grant access to the Dubai Aquarium.

If you'd like to take a break, you can relax at the "Atmosphere" café on the 122nd floor of the Burj Khalifa. Here, you can enjoy delicious food and drinks while taking in the view of the city and beyond. Please remember to make a reservation in advance, as this spot is very popular.

End your visit by stopping at the souvenir shop on the ground floor to pick up a memento of this extraordinary day. You'll find a selection of exclusive souvenirs, ranging from artwork to models of the Burj Khalifa.

Good to Know

The "At the Top SKY" ticket (floors 124+125+148) costs approximately £85. The regular "At the Top" ticket (floors 124+125) is around £35. The combo ticket (floors 124+125 and Dubai Aquarium) is priced at about £50. All ticket options can easily be purchased online at www.burjkhalifa.ae.

How to Get There?

Nearby Metro Station:

Burj Khalifa/Dubai Mall

2h Dubai Downtown

The Dubai Fountain Show is located in front of the iconic Burj Khalifa, in the heart of Downtown Dubai. The show takes place in a man-made lake that spans a remarkable area. The fountains shoot up in sync with the rhythm of the music and are illuminated by colorful lights.

Designed by a renowned California-based company, also responsible for the famous fountains at the Bellagio Hotel in Las Vegas, the Dubai Fountain shines amidst numerous lights and color projectors. Stretching a total length of 275 meters, the water shoots up to around 150 meters high and is accompanied by a variety of music styles. The carefully selected music is harmoniously synchronized with the water movements, enhancing the visual experience. During the show, playful lights around the fountains change colors, adding an extra dimension.

DUBAI FOUNTAIN SHOW

Experience a Spectacular Water Show

There are several spots from which you can admire the Dubai Fountain Show. A popular option is the promenade along the artificial lake, which offers close proximity to the fountains for an immersive experience. Another great vantage point is the upper deck of the Dubai Mall, where you can take in the entire show while also enjoying views of the surrounding skyline.

If you plan to visit the Dubai Fountain Show, we recommend arriving early to secure a good spot. The show's popularity draws large crowds, and arriving in advance ensures you have an optimal view of the spectacle. You can also combine your visit with other activities, as the Dubai Fountain Show is located near many additional attractions. A stroll through the Dubai Mall or a relaxing dinner at one of the nearby restaurants can enhance your overall experience.

The Dubai Fountain Show at Night

Good to Know

Admission to the Dubai Fountain Show is free. Performances take place daily from 6:00 PM to 11:00 PM at intervals of about 30 minutes. Additionally, there are midday shows at 1:00 PM and 1:30 PM (and at 2:00 PM on Fridays). The show itself lasts about 5 minutes.

How to Get There?

Nearby Metro Station:

Burj Khalifa/Dubai Mall

The Underwater Tunnel at the Dubai Aquarium

#3

2h

Discover Dubai's Mysterious Depths

UP CLOSE AT THE DUBAI AQUARIUM

The Dubai Aquarium is not just an aquarium but an extraordinary underwater landscape that blurs the boundaries between the world above and below the water. As one of the largest indoor aquariums in the world, it amazes visitors with an incredible variety of marine life. But it's not just about observing – it's about diving into the vibrant heart of the oceans.

Did you know that the aquarium is home to more than 140 species of marine life, including over 300 sharks and rays? The main tank, which holds more than 10 million liters of water, is home to majestic sand tiger sharks and graceful stingrays. But there's more than just fish – the underwater world also features coral reefs, offering a colorful home to a wide variety of creatures.

The absolute highlight of the aquarium is undoubtedly the impressive underwater tunnel. When you walk through this tunnel, you will feel like you are in the middle of the sea. Sharks glide majestically above you as you take in the fascinating marine world up close.

For the brave adventurers among you, shark diving offers the chance to dive in a special cage right in the middle of the main tank. From this secure position, you'll be surrounded by sharks and other marine creatures. If you're looking for an unforgettable

Shark Diving at the Dubai Aquarium

The Dubai Aquarium in the Dubai Mall

A Shark in the Underwater Tunnel

adventure without needing diving experience, Cage Snorkeling provides the perfect opportunity. You can snorkel in a safe cage within the main tank and experience the impressive marine world up close.

For those who want to enjoy the underwater world without getting wet, a glass-bottom boat tour is the perfect option. Step into a boat with a clear glass floor and be enchanted by the stunning views of the diverse marine life and vibrant reefs beneath you.

At the Dubai Aquarium, you can even interact with penguins. During the "Penguin Encounters", you have the chance to get closer to the penguins, observe them, and even take photos with them. The experience is often accompanied by expert animal keepers who provide information about the penguins and can answer your questions. Additionally, you have the opportunity to interact not only with penguins but also with a 750 kg King Crocodile, otters, or rays.

The Dubai Aquarium offers a wide range of activities for all ages and interests. Whether you are an adventurer, a knowledge seeker, or simply curious, you will surely find an activity here that ignites your passion for the magnificent world of the seas.

Good to Know

The Dubai Aquarium & Underwater Zoo is located in the Dubai Mall and can be viewed from the outside for free. It is open daily from 10:00 AM to 11:00 PM, and on weekends, the aquarium stays open until midnight. The cheapest ticket for the Dubai Aquarium & Underwater Zoo costs approximately £40 per person and includes access to the Aquarium Tunnel, the Underwater Zoo, the Penguin Encounter, a small tour, and a £5 voucher each for the Aquarium Café and Aquarium Shop. There are various premium and VIP ticket options (it's worth checking the website to find the best ticket option for you: www.thedubaiaquarium.com). Shark diving and snorkeling each cost around £85 per person.

How to Get There?

Nearby Metro Station:

Burj Khalifa/Dubai Mall

The Waterfall in the Dubai Mall

Shop, Dine, and Enjoy Unforgettable Flavors at the DUBAI MALL

The Dubai Mall, one of the largest shopping centers in the world, awaits you with an impressive variety of entertainment, shopping options, and culinary delights. With over 1,200 stores across various sectors, from fashion and electronics to handicrafts, the mall offers a wide range of products to suit every taste and need.

What will immediately catch your eye in the Dubai Mall is the previously mentioned Dubai Aquarium, an astonishing underwater world that

Gold Souk in the Dubai Mall

Atrium of the Dubai Mall

you can experience up close. If you're interested in high-end fashion and designer brands, the Fashion Avenue in the Dubai Mall is the place for you. From world-renowned fashion designers to exclusive jewelry stores, you'll find everything here to make the heart of any fashion enthusiast skip a beat. The Dubai Mall is not only a paradise for shopaholics but also a culinary hub of the highest caliber. The selection of restaurants, cafés, and food courts is impressive, offering a global variety of flavors. Whether you're looking for international delicacies or regional specialties, you're sure to find something to satisfy your taste buds here.

The Dubai Mall also offers an extensive range of entertainment for families. "KidZania Dubai" allows children to immerse themselves in a miniature city and explore various professions through play. Additionally, the "VR Park Dubai" provides virtual adventures for all ages, from thrilling roller coaster rides to interactive games.

If you visit the Dubai Mall early in the morning, not only will you avoid the crowds, but you can also take advantage of special breakfast offers in selected shops. A hidden gem is the "Dubai Dino" located in the Gold Souk area of the Dubai Mall. Here, you can admire the impressive skeleton of a massive dinosaur – a must-see for history and dinosaur enthusiasts.

The "Dubai Dino" in the Dubai Mall

DUBA
MALL

There is also an ice rink located right in the middle of the Dubai Mall. The rink spans a generous area, providing ample space for both beginners and experienced skaters to enjoy themselves. Whether you're taking your first steps on the ice or showcasing your figure skating skills, the ice rink offers a welcoming environment for all skill levels.

If you've ever wanted to fly an airplane, you can do so in one of the best flight simulators at the Dubai Mall. The Emirates A380 simulator offers an unforgettable adventure high above the clouds, giving you the experience of piloting one of the world's largest aircraft.

In the bustling Dubai Mall, visitors also have the opportunity to take a detour to Chinatown. This unique area immerses you in the rich culture, delicious food, and vibrant atmosphere of an authentic Chinese neighborhood. A highlight of Chinatown is undoubtedly its culinary diversity. From delectable dim sum and fresh dumplings to flavorful stir-fry dishes, the restaurants and food stalls offer a comprehensive range of Chinese cuisine. Here, you can savor the flavors of China without ever leaving the Dubai Mall.

Good to Know

The Dubai Mall is open daily from 10:00 AM to 11:00 PM, and from Friday to Sunday until midnight (for more information, visit www.thedubaimall.com).

How to Get There?

Nearby Metro Station:

Burj Khalifa/Dubai Mall

Dubai Mall

Dubai Opera

#5

4h

Experience a Magical Evening of Music at the **DUBAI OPERA**

The Dubai Opera, which opened in 2016, offers music enthusiasts an impressive experience. Nestled in the heart of Dubai's cultural district and within sight of the majestic Burj Khalifa, its location is truly unique and promises an unforgettable experience.

The architecture of the Dubai Opera is reminiscent of a traditional Arabian dhow ship, yet it blends seamlessly into the modern skyline. Its glass facade offers a unique view of Burj Lake and the vibrant skyline. The location allows visitors to enjoy world-class performances while also admiring the enchanting fountain show on Burj Lake.

The variety of events and programs at the Dubai Opera is extensive. Operas, ballets, concerts, plays, and comedy shows all find their stage here. This diverse program attracts both local and international artists. Visitors are expected to follow a dress code and proper etiquette. Elegant attire is recommended to respect the sophisticated atmosphere, allowing all guests

Dubai Opera
at Night

to contribute to a respectful environment. The Dubai Opera also offers culinary delights, with various restaurants and lounges inviting guests to relax before or after the show. Here, you can enjoy exquisite meals and drinks, completing the overall experience.

For visitors who don't wish to attend a performance, the Dubai Opera Tour is a great option. The futuristic building is worth a visit in its own right, and on a guided tour, you'll receive fascinating insights into the history and architecture of the opera house.

To secure the best view of the stage, we recommend booking tickets early, especially for events featuring prominent artists, as seats tend to sell out quickly.

Good to Know

The Dubai Opera operates according to its event schedule. Ticket prices vary depending on the event and seating, typically ranging between approximately £45 and £170 (for more information, visit www.dubaiopera.com). A Dubai Opera Tour costs around £35 per person and can be booked through providers such as GetYourGuide (www.getyourguide.com).

How to Get There?

Nearby Metro Station:

Burj Khalifa/Dubai Mall

Dubai Opera

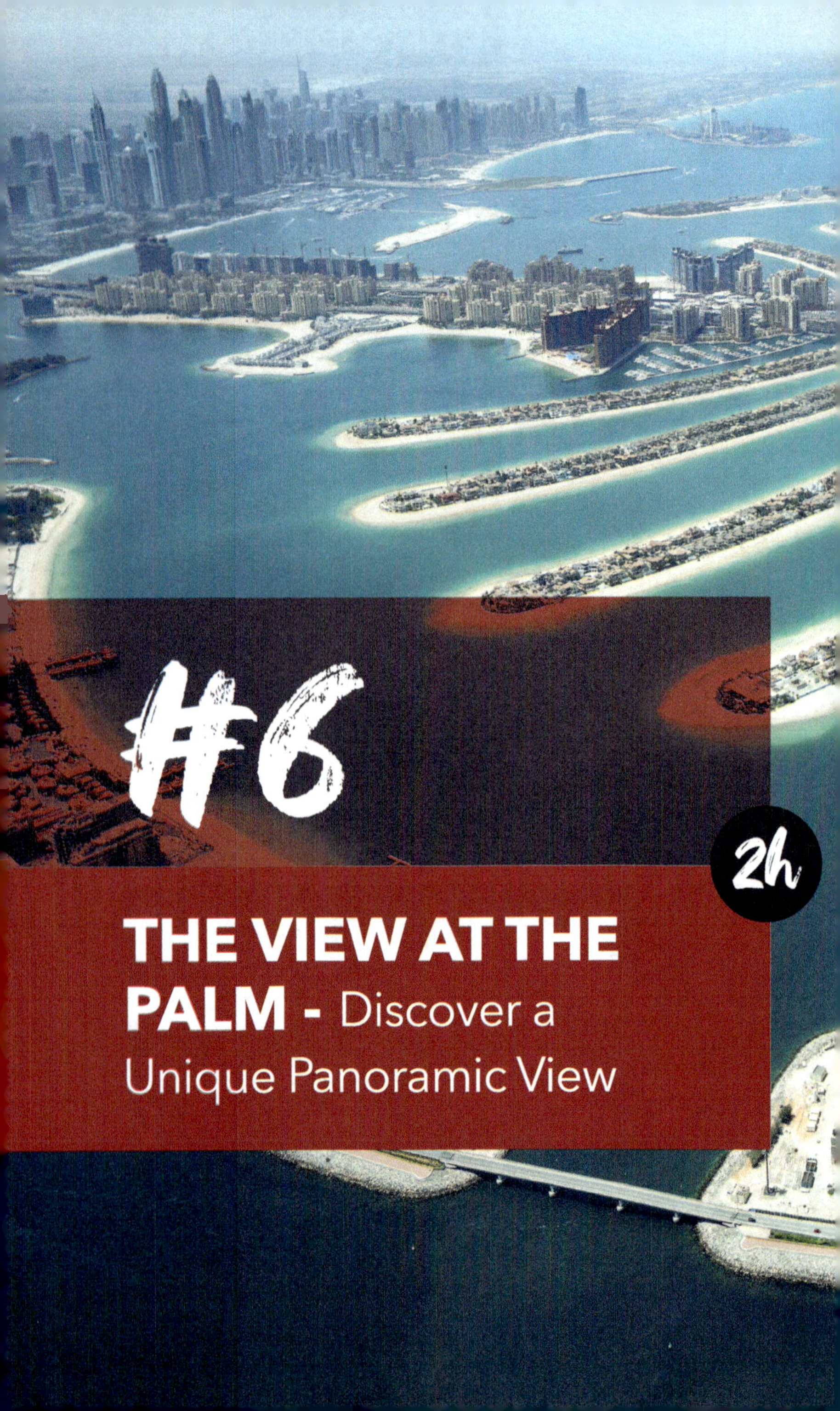

#6

2h

THE VIEW AT THE PALM - Discover a Unique Panoramic View

Palm Jumeirah

Located on the 52nd floor of St. Regis Dubai - The Palm, "The View at The Palm" offers an incredible 360-degree view of the city and the sea.

A visit to "The View at The Palm" at a height of 240 meters is an absolute highlight. From here, you truly grasp the immense scale of the artificial Palm Island. In the past, visitors had to rely on hotels with good views to recognize the shape of the palm, but now "The View at The Palm" offers an unparalleled panoramic view, making this experience unforgettable.

The moment the elevator doors open and you step onto the observation deck, you'll be rewarded with a breathtaking view of Dubai's expansive skyline. In front of you, skyscrapers, islands, and a coastline defined by modern architecture and urban elegance stretch as far as the eye can see. The

clear view extends to the distant horizon of the Persian Gulf. Visit "The View at The Palm" in the late afternoon to witness the spectacular sunset over Dubai. The setting sun bathes the skyline in a warm, golden light, casting a magical glow over the city. As night falls, the twinkling city lights create an equally impressive display.

Whether for a romantic date, a special occasion, a gathering with friends, or a family reunion, we highly recommend the rooftop restaurant "CouCou Dubai" when you visit "The View at The Palm". Relax on the comfortable lounge seating and indulge in Mediterranean delicacies, exotic cocktails, or even a shisha if you desire. CouCou Dubai is not just a place to enjoy food but also a venue of elegance. Here, you'll experience an unparalleled view of Palm Jumeirah and Dubai's coastline. The combination of sophisticated interiors, exquisite haute cuisine made from the finest ingredients, exceptional service, and a captivating atmosphere will exceed your expectations.

Palm Jumeirah

Good to Know

"The View at The Palm" is open daily from 10:00 AM to 8:00 PM. The entrance fee is more affordable compared to the Burj Khalifa. Adults pay approximately £20, and children around £15. During the popular prime hours from 4:00 PM to 7:00 PM, tickets cost about £34 for adults and £25 for children (more information can be found at www.theview-palm.ae). The building is located at Nakheel Mall on Palm Jumeirah.

You can get there by taxi, rental car, or the monorail (stop at "Shopping Mall").

How to Get There?

Nearby Metro Station:

Shopping Mall

#7

2h

An exquisite 7-star luxury tour at the

BURJ AL ARAB

Experience a one-of-a-kind Burj Al Arab tour and explore the luxurious world of one of the most exclusive hotels. The self-proclaimed 7-star hotel, Burj Al Arab, also known as the "Tower of the Arabs", rises majestically to a height of 321 meters above Dubai's impressive skyline and stands as an iconic landmark of the city.

The Burj Al Arab was designed with a sail-shaped structure, symbolizing both Dubai's past as a maritime trading hub and the city's forward-looking vision. This unique building sits on an artificial island off the coast and is anchored to the seabed by massive support piles, extending up to 45 meters deep into the ocean floor.

Every surface inside the Burj Al Arab exudes an aura of unparalleled luxury. Nearly 2,000 square meters of 24-carat gold leaf were used to adorn the hotel's interior. But that's not all – on the ceiling of the Japanese restaurant Junsui, no fewer than 21,000 glittering Swarovski crystals decorate the

The Burj Al Arab from the Inside

Luxurious Suite
in the Burj Al Arab

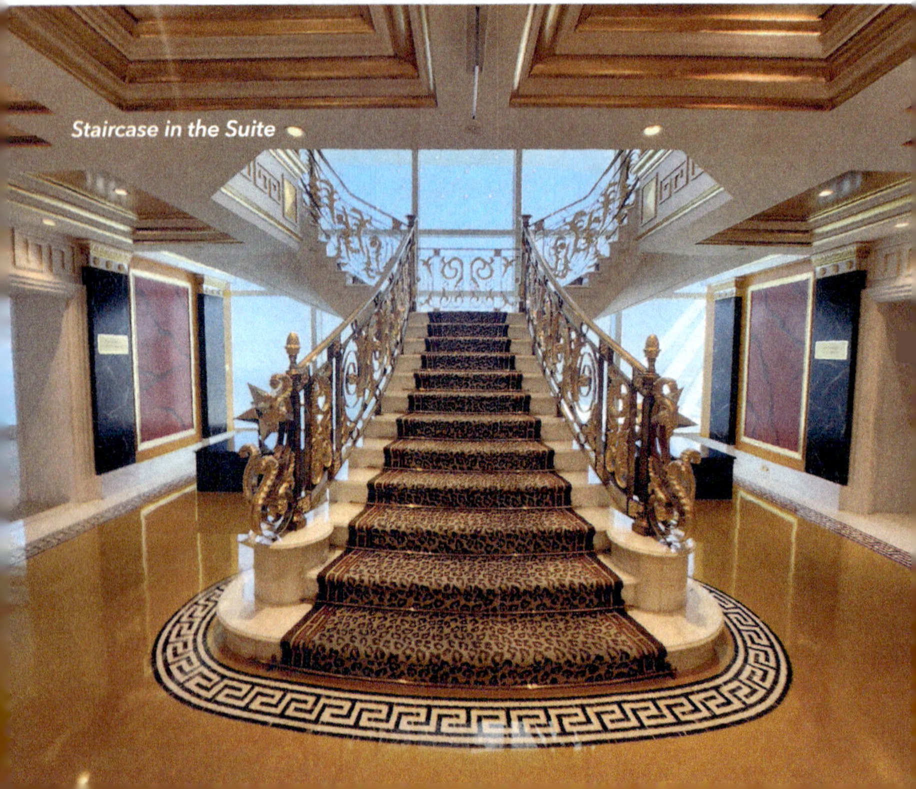
Staircase in the Suite

room, creating a truly magnificent "starry sky" of impressive scale. Additionally, the majority of the floors and walls in the Burj Al Arab are crafted from exclusive Italian Statuario marble, the same marble Michelangelo used for his masterpieces.

The Burj Al Arab offers its discerning guests 202 luxurious suites, each consisting solely of spacious accommodations ranging from 169 to 780 square meters. Every suite is a masterpiece in itself, offering spectacular views of the azure sea and the surrounding skyline. Guests are pampered with Rolls-Royce and helicopter transfers to make their journey even more comfortable.

The helipad of the Burj Al Arab is just as impressive as the hotel itself. In 2005, tennis stars Roger Federer and Andre Agassi played a match atop the helipad. A year earlier, Tiger Woods hit a golf ball from the same spot, a feat later repeated by Rory McIlroy. In 2017, professional kitesurfer Nick Jacobsen pulled off an incredible stunt by jumping off the Burj Al Arab's helipad with a kiteboard.

The Burj Al Arab tour promises an extraordinary experience for visitors. Begin your journey with a warm welcome drink and a relaxed buggy ride over the bridge to Burj Al Arab Island. The panoramic elevator will then take you to the 25th floor, where a breathtaking view of Dubai and the surrounding coastline unfolds. Next, explore the opulent Experience Suite and be mesmerized by the beauty of the panoramic landscape. The tour then takes you to the lavish Royal Suite, which embodies luxury and elegance at its finest. In the exclusive boutique, you can purchase exquisite souvenirs to make your visit unforgettable. To top off the experience, indulge in a delightful Gold Cappuccino in the UMA Lounge, a treat that will truly satisfy your senses.

Good to Know

The Burj Al Arab tour, including a Gold Cappuccino, costs around £85 per person (more information available at www.insideburjalarab.com). The tour is available daily from 10:00 AM to 6:30 PM.

How to Get There?

Mashreq

Take the metro to Mashreq Station, then you can catch bus line 81 to the Burj Al Arab Hotel 2 station. From there, it's about a 10-minute walk to the Burj Al Arab.

2h Jumeirah

#8

2h

Discover the Legend of Atlantis at the LOST CHAMBERS AQUARIUM

The Lost Chambers Aquarium is more than just an aquarium – it's a tribute to the lost city of Atlantis, whose legend is deeply rooted in ancient mythology.

Here, visitors encounter a unique blend of mystical history and fascinating marine biology. The thoughtfully designed space gives the impression of walking through the remnants of this lost civilization. This enigmatic attraction is located in the magnificent Atlantis The Palm Hotel, right next to the Aquaventure Waterpark on Palm Jumeirah Island, and promises hours of entertainment for every guest.

Your adventure at the Lost Chambers Aquarium begins with a walk through the massive tanks, meticulously designed to showcase the underwater world in all its glory. Admire an astonishing variety of marine life – from vibrant tropical fish to majestic rays and even sharks. The impressive viewing windows allow you to immerse

Lost Chambers Aquarium

yourself in the perspective of the sea creatures and experience their natural habitats up close.

At the Lost Chambers Aquarium, certified divers have the unique opportunity to dive into the breathtaking underwater world of the 10-meters-deep Ambassador Lagoon. The Ambassador Lagoon is the largest of all the aquarium environments in the Lost Chambers. During the dive, you can interact directly with a variety of small and large marine creatures. It's important to note that this dive is specifically designed for certified divers. If you're interested in participating in this extraordinary experience, make sure to book in advance and ensure that you have the necessary diving certifications and skills.

For non-certified divers, there are plenty of activities to enjoy as well. The Ambassador Lagoon offers exciting snorkeling experiences and the adventurous Shark Safari. During the Shark Safari, you'll descend to the bottom of the aquarium and walk among sharks, rays, and various other fish on the sandy floor. You'll be equipped with special diving gear and a large glass helmet that provides ample oxygen, allowing you to breathe comfortably while exploring this underwater world.

The Lost Chambers Aquarium is slightly smaller than the Dubai Aquarium & Underwater Zoo in the Dubai Mall, but due to its mythical atmosphere and beautiful design both inside and outside the tanks, it's definitely worth a visit. The aquarium evokes the legend of the lost city of Atlantis and is designed in the form of tunnels and mazes. As you explore, you'll discover an impressive underwater world where more than 65,000 marvelous marine creatures swim around.

The aquariums at the Lost Chambers are uniquely illuminated, allowing the marine life to be showcased in all its splendor. For the ultimate Atlantis experience, it's highly recommended to join one of the Myth Tours, which take place hourly. During these tours, you'll learn all about the lost city of Atlantis and the thousands of animals living in the aquarium.

Good to Know

The aquarium is open daily from 10:00 AM to 9:00 PM. Tickets for the Lost Chambers Aquarium alone cost approximately £25. A regular day pass for the Aquaventure Waterpark, located at the same site, costs about £65, and with access to the Lost Chambers Aquarium, it's around £75. We recommend combining the aquarium with the Aquaventure Waterpark, as the aquarium entry is only an additional £8. A certified dive costs around £220 per person, snorkeling about £100, and the Shark Safari approximately £135 per person. All tickets can easily be reserved online at www.atlantis.com.

How to Get There?

Aquaventure Waterpark

We recommend arriving by taxi or rental car to the Atlantis The Palm Hotel. Alternatively, you can take the monorail to the Aquaventure Waterpark station.

#9

Learn More About the Cultural Significance of the JUMEIRAH MOSQUE

2h

Since its grand opening in 1979, the magnificent Jumeirah Mosque stands as a gift from the late Sheikh Rashid bin Saeed Al Maktoum, the former ruler of Dubai.

The mosque, inspired by the distant lands of Syria and Egypt, impresses not only with its majestic presence but also with its capacity to welcome around 1,500 worshippers within its walls. However, the Jumeirah Mosque is more than just a place of worship – it is a symbol of cultural bridge-building and mutual understanding. For over two decades, the Jumeirah Mosque has been a central hub for the "Open Doors, Open Minds" program. Here, you have the opportunity to engage with your guide, ask extensive questions, and take remarkable photos. Join a tour of this iconic mosque – one of the most popular mosque visits in Dubai, warmly welcoming non-Muslims as well.

An unforgettable experience awaits visitors right from the moment they register on-site. Here, you can look forward to a selection of light yet authentic Emirati refreshments. It's recommended to arrive at least 30 minutes before the program begins to fully enjoy this exciting journey into the world of culture and history. Refreshments such as Arabic coffee, tea,

Jumeirah Moschee

Interior of the Jumeirah Mosque

Hospitality at the Mosque

dates, water, and the delicious Lokma (sweet Arabic dough balls) are served, allowing you to immerse yourself in local hospitality even before the program officially starts.

In addition to an authentic mosque visit, the tour also takes you on a journey back in time at the "Once Upon a Time Museum", where you'll step into the 1970s and 1980s. Rare artifacts and vintage items have been carefully curated to give you the sense of being transported to past eras. Furthermore, you'll gain insights into the accompanying World Gallery, explore local henna art, or capture a memorable photo with a majestic falcon.

To visit the Jumeirah Mosque, it is recommended to wear appropriate clothing – long pants and covered shoulders for men, and women should wear a headscarf to cover their hair. If you don't have suitable attire with you, it can be provided at the entrance.

For all culturally interested travelers, Dubai offers a wealth of other impressive mosques, such as the Al-Farooq Mosque and the Grand Mosque in Bur Dubai. A trip to Abu Dhabi to visit the Sheikh Zayed Mosque is also highly recommended.

Good to Know

The public tours of the Jumeirah Mosque take place from Saturday to Thursday and cost approximately £9 per person. There are two tours each day, with the first starting at 10:00 AM and the second at 2:00 PM. On-site registration begins 30 minutes before the tour (for more information, visit www.jumeirahmosque.ae).

How to Get There?

Business Bay or Max

From the Business Bay Metro Station, take bus line 9 to the Palm Strip Center stop. From the Max Metro Station, you can take bus line X28 to the Jumeirah, Grand Masjid stop.

Original Pages of the Constitution

#10

2h

A VISIT TO THE ETIHAD MUSEUM

A Journey Through the Founding of the UAE

At the beautifully designed Etihad Museum on Jumeirah Road, not far from the Jumeirah Mosque, you have the opportunity to explore the fascinating story of the founding of the United Arab Emirates on December 2, 1971, as well as the rich history of Dubai.

This history is closely tied to the discovery of oil in the 1950s and the subsequent withdrawal of the British in 1968. This extraordinary museum captivates visitors with documentaries, photographs, artifacts, timelines, and interactive exhibits that highlight the historical milestones before and after this significant event, paying tribute to the seven founding fathers of the nation. The museum itself, designed by a Canadian architectural firm, impresses with its elegant architecture. The roof symbolizes the paper on which the declaration was written, while the seven golden columns in the entrance hall represent the pens used to sign it. A beautiful white limestone plaza connects the building with the historic round Union House and the reconstructed guesthouse where the founding fathers stayed during the negotiations. Above a reflecting pool stands the original flagpole, where the rulers gathered after signing the agreement. Naturally, the museum also highlights the immense growth Dubai has experienced over the past 20 years.

A significant part of the museum complex is the restored Union House, where the leaders of the Emirates founded the United Arab Emirates in 1971. Although the Union House was completely destroyed at the time, a large portion of it can now be visited thanks to the restoration efforts.

In the spacious underground galleries, which you access via a striking white marble staircase, you'll encounter a wide range of impressive exhibits. Admire the gigantic painting by Emirati artist Abdul Qader Al Rais, which depicts the geography of the UAE. Right next to it, you'll find remarkable photographs of the rulers of the seven Emirates who founded the nation, along with their family trees and personal items such as Sheikh Zayed's walking stick and sunglasses, and Sheikh Rashid's passport. Special 3D documentaries about the founding years, as well as the original first page of the Constitution, are further highlights of the Etihad Museum. By the way, the name of the museum has no connection to the airline of the same name; "Etihad" simply means "Union" in Arabic.

Good to Know

The Etihad Museum is open daily from 10:00 AM to 8:00 PM. Admission costs approximately £6 for adults, £3 for children and youth (ages 5-24), and around £2 for children under 5 years old.

How to Get There?

Business Bay

From the Business Bay Metro Station, take bus line 9 to the Etihad Museum 2 stop.

#11

2h

OSSIANO RESTAURANT

Underwater Romance and Haute Cuisine in Perfection

The Ossiano Restaurant captivates with its exceptional location and interior design. Set against the backdrop of one of the largest and most impressive aquariums in the world, Ossiano is considered one of the most romantic underwater restaurants globally.

While you dine, sharks, stingrays, and numerous other fish swim right by your table. The large dining room features floor-to-ceiling glass walls, offering a direct view of the water and ensuring a magical dining experience. Divers can even be hired to deliver underwater love notes or marriage proposals. The concept and atmosphere of Ossiano Restaurant have evolved over time. In recent years, a more relaxed, contemporary approach has been introduced. Tablecloths were removed, and a DJ now provides soft deep-house beats during the meal. The breathtaking views remain, enhanced by subtle, luxurious lighting and ample space.

At Ossiano, guests enjoy a fine dining experience where top-quality ingredients are at the heart of every dish. The cuisine is modern and visually stunning, with flavor always taking precedence. Multi-course tasting menus offer a culinary rollercoaster. While the foundation of the cooking is often traditional, the execution is contemporary. For instance, Iranian caviar is served alongside French truffles and langoustines from the North Sea. As long as it's of the highest quality, it can and will be served. Ossiano's strong relationships with Dubai's best suppliers ensure consistently top-notch ingredients.

Sustainability is another hallmark of the restaurant's kitchen. Every part of an ingredient is utilized – if not consumed, it is transformed into broth or amuse-bouche, keeping waste levels remarkably low. Ossiano can best be described as international fine dining, where the stories behind the dishes and the artistic table presentations elevate the meal.

Ossiano is among the top fine dining restaurants in Dubai. More than just a restaurant, it offers an exquisite culinary experience, combining a magical underwater setting with some of the finest dishes in the world.

Good to Know

Ossiano is open from Tuesday to Sunday, 6:00 PM to 1:00 AM. The dress code is elegant, and children aged 10 and above are welcome. Ossiano holds a Michelin star, and the prices reflect its fine dining status. The 11-course Michelin-starred menu costs around £250 per person (for more information and reservations, visit www.atlantis.com).

How to Get There?

We recommend arriving by taxi or rental car to Atlantis The Palm Hotel.

#12

2h

XLINE DUBAI

Fly Through the Dubai Marina on the World's Fastest Zipline

The XLine Dubai Zipline is one of the longest urban ziplines in the world and is located in the heart of Dubai.

The zipline at Dubai Marina has even broken world records, being the steepest and fastest zipline ever. Spanning over a kilometer, with a 16-degree incline and an average speed of 80 km/h, you'll soar into breathtaking views of the Dubai Marina, surrounded by luxurious 5-star hotels, shopping malls, and yachts. The organizers of XLine Dubai Zipline prioritize safety and comfort. All equipment is regularly maintained and inspected to ensure the highest safety standards. Before your ride, you'll receive a thorough briefing on the proper use of the equipment and safety measures.

After the briefing, you'll ascend to the rooftop, approximately 170 meter high, where your zipline adventure will begin. During the ascent, you can already catch a glimpse of the incredible city views that await you during the ride. Once you reach the starting point, the guides will carefully secure you into your zipline harness and ensure everything is fastened safely. At this moment, you may feel a rush of excitement and anticipation, as the thrill of the upcoming ride builds up.

With a confident leap or gentle push, you'll be released and soar at breathtaking speed along the zipline. The wind rushes around you as you fly over Dubai's skyline. The speed and thrill are unmatched, and the unique perspective of the city below is truly awe-inspiring. Additionally, GoPro cameras attached to your helmet will capture the entire ride, allowing you to relive the exhilarating experience.

Please note that to ride the XLine Dubai Zipline, you must be between 12 and 65 years old and have a minimum height of 130 cm. Your weight should be between 45 and 100 kg, and you should be physically fit.

Good to Know

Tickets cost approximately £140 per person, while children under 16 pay around £110 (more information available at www.xdubai.com). The XLine is open from Wednesday to Monday, between 9:20 AM and 11:20 AM, and from 3:20 PM to 6:20 PM. Hours may vary depending on the season, so it's worth checking the website beforehand.

How to get There?

DMCC

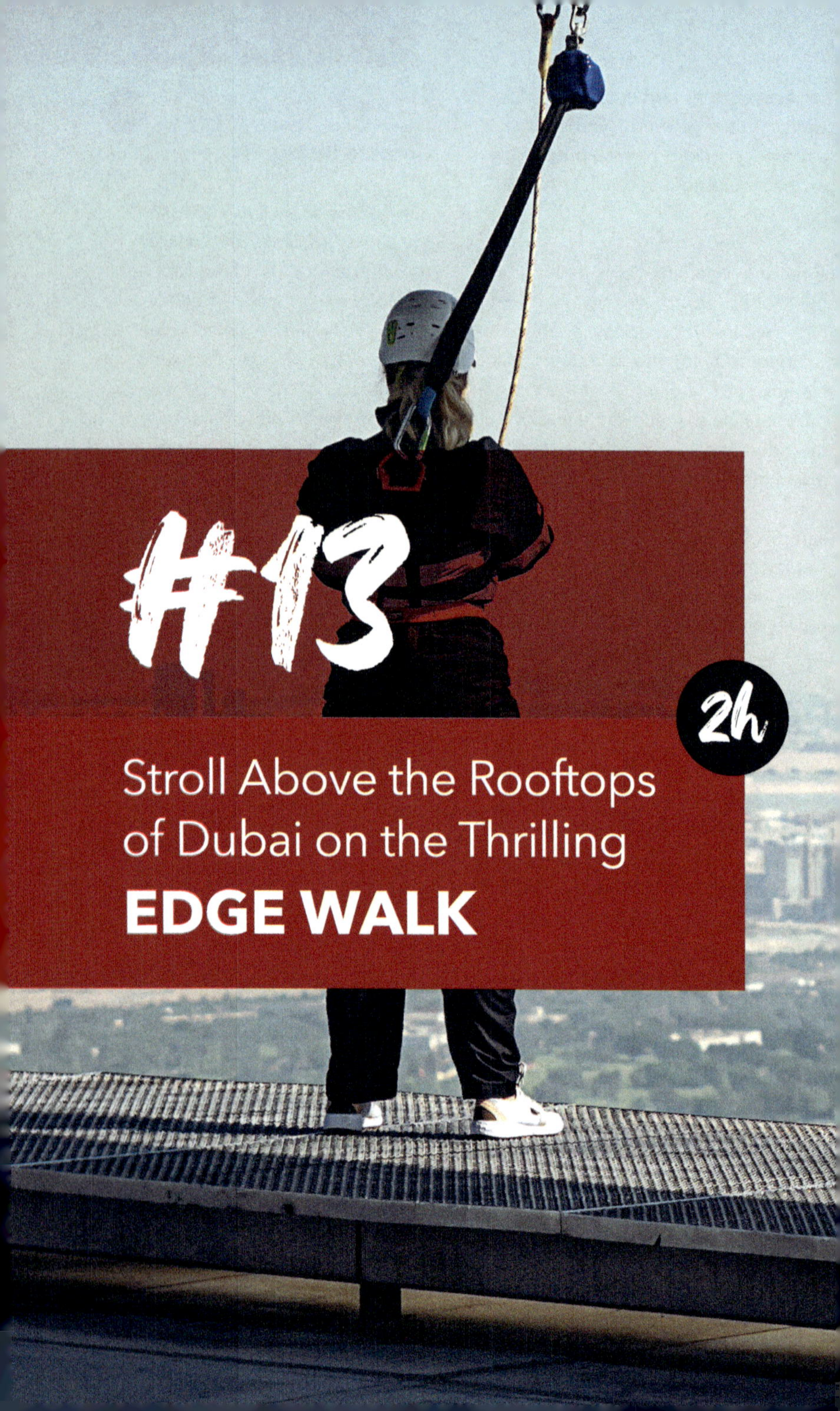

#13

2h

Stroll Above the Rooftops of Dubai on the Thrilling **EDGE WALK**

Have you ever dreamed of defying gravity, letting adrenaline flow through your veins and conquering your fears? Look no further – the Edge Walk at Sky Views Dubai is the perfect adventure for you.

This thrilling experience allows you to see Dubai from an entirely new perspective as you walk along the outer edge of one of the world's most impressive skyscrapers.

Before embarking on the Edge Walk, you will be welcomed by professional guides who provide a comprehensive safety briefing. You'll receive detailed instructions on using the equipment, which is specifically designed for this adventure.

During the Edge Walk, you'll have the opportunity to view Dubai from a completely new perspective. The city's extraordinary skyline stretching to the horizon, the shimmering waters of the Arabian Gulf, and the futuristic skyscrapers will leave you breathless. As you move slowly along the edge, you'll feel the gentle wind brush across your face. The sounds of the city become distant echoes, and time seems to stand still. The combination of adrenaline and spectacular views makes this activity an unforgettable experience during your Dubai trip.

Good to Know

The Edge Walk costs approximately £110 per person (more information available at www.skyviews-dubai.com) and is available daily from 10:30 AM to 8:30 PM.

How to Get There?

Burj Khalifa / Dubai Mall

#14

2h

Create Your Own Perfume at **VILLA 515**

Villa 515 serves as both a cozy café and an exceptional perfumery, frequented by lovers of fine fragrances.

Along Jumeirah Beach Road, one would never expect to find this beautiful garden hidden behind its walls. But once you step into this secret world of scents, it feels like entering a small wonderland. The perfumery houses fragrances from world-renowned perfumers, which can be purchased. Additionally, there is a lab for personalized perfume consultations.

Since 2013, Villa 515 has offered an oasis for fragrance enthusiasts seeking a unique and creative journey. Founded by passionate perfume connoisseurs, the charming Arabian villa presents a rich selection of niche fragrances. The interior was designed by Lilian Driessen, a Dutch fashion designer, while the diverse range of scents is crafted by Alessandro Gualtieri, a creative Italian perfume director. Villa 515 invites you to enjoy the dreamy setting and even create your own unique fragrance in the perfume lab. From selecting top niche brands to learning about raw materials through various courses and workshops, an extraordinary experience awaits you here.

The accompanying café, both indoors and in the outdoor garden, invites you to sit down and enjoy drinks along with savory or sweet treats. The delicious desserts come with a local twist, such as a homemade peanut brownie or an exquisite saffron cigar. Villa 515 is truly an extraordinary place, standing out from the usual suspects among perfumeries and cafés. Who knows, maybe you'll create your own unique perfume at Villa 515, one that exists nowhere else in the world…

Good to Know

Villa 515 is open daily from 8:00 AM to 10:00 PM. Perfume prices start at approximately £65 (more information available at www.villa515.com).

How to Get There?

Bus line N55 stops directly in front of Villa 515. Get off at the Jumeirah 3, Masjid 2 stop.

4h Jumeirah

#15

4h

JUMEIRAH BEACH

Relax on One of Dubai's Most Beautiful Beaches

Jumeirah Beach is the most well-known and popular beach in Dubai. Located just a few kilometers from the city, it stretches about 30 km along the coast.

With its white, fine-grained sand and stunning views of the iconic Burj Al Arab, it invites visitors to enjoy relaxing days by the sea. However, Jumeirah Beach offers much more than just sun and sand.

For those looking for accommodations directly on Jumeirah Beach, there are various luxury hotels to choose from. These offer everything from exquisite rooms with sea views to top-notch amenities. Particularly exclusive are the private beach sections, providing guests with a serene and secluded environment for uninterrupted relaxation.

Jumeirah Beach Park, on the other hand, is an excellent choice for families and nature lovers. For a small fee of around £2, visitors gain access to top-notch facilities such as showers, changing rooms, restrooms, and kiosks. In addition, there are playgrounds for children, a spacious park, and barbecue areas that can be freely used. The park provides the perfect setting for a picnic or to watch the sunset over the sparkling sea.

For those who prefer not to pay an entry fee, Jumeirah Public Beach is an excellent alternative. It's part of Jumeirah Beach and offers free access to the beach. Here, you can enjoy the warm, clear waters of the Persian Gulf and take leisurely strolls along the shore. Jumeirah Public Beach is popular with both locals and tourists alike, offering a lively and social atmosphere.

Jumeirah Beach is also a paradise for water sports enthusiasts. Sailing, water skiing, diving, and many other activities are available to make your day exciting and diverse. The local water sports centers offer courses and rental options for all skill levels. An adventure on the water promises to be an unforgettable experience that visitors can fully enjoy.

Good to Know

Jumeirah Beach is open 24/7. Admission to Jumeirah Beach Park is approximately £2 per person, while access to Jumeirah Public Beach is free.

How to Get There?

Mashreq or Max

From Mashreq or Max Metro Stations, take one of the many bus connections to Jumeirah Beach Park (Mashreq: bus line 81) or Jumeirah Public Beach (Max: bus line X28).

Imagine stepping out of the scorching heat of Dubai and suddenly finding yourself in a winter oasis. A cool breeze brushes against your face as you gaze upon the sparkling snow, feeling the refreshing tingle of ice crystals on your skin.

Sounds unbelievable? But it's a reality at the incredible Ski Dubai in the Mall of the Emirates, which, with its more than 400 shops and alpine-style restaurants, is unique in the world. Inside this impressive ski hall, you can ski, snowboard, and sled all year round – a refreshing escape from the hot temperatures outside.

The main attraction at Ski Dubai is undoubtedly the 85-meter-high indoor ski slope, suitable for skiers and snowboarders of all levels. From beginners to experienced riders, everyone can enjoy the fun. The slope is covered with real snow, offering an authentic skiing experience in cool sub-zero

#16

4h

SKI DUBAI

A Touch of Winter in the Middle of the Desert

4h Jumeirah

temperatures. Thanks to state-of-the-art snow machines, the perfect snow quality is maintained throughout the year.

If you're stepping onto skis for the first time or trying your hand at snowboarding, Ski Dubai offers qualified instructors to guide you through the basics. A dedicated beginner area allows newcomers to take their first steps on the snow in a safe environment. More advanced riders can look forward to challenging slopes and exciting turns.

View into Ski Dubai from the Mall of the Emirates

Winter Wonderland in the Heart of the Desert

Ski Dubai provides everything you need for your snow adventure. From skis and snowboards to winter clothing and gear, you'll find it all to be fully equipped for the slopes. All you need to bring is your enthusiasm!

In addition to the slope, Ski Dubai offers a snow park with numerous activities such as sledding, bobsledding, igloo building, snowball fights, and even exploring an ice cave. This is a fun addition for families with children, adding variety to skiing.

One of the most extraordinary experiences at Ski Dubai is the chance to meet the resident penguins. You'll have the opportunity to observe these charming creatures up close and even participate in a guided tour. Experienced caretakers will share

interesting facts about the penguins, and you'll get the chance to touch them and take photos, making it a truly memorable experience.

After an exciting day on the slopes, you can relax in the cozy après-ski chalets and alpine-style restaurants along the edge of the piste. Here, you can warm up with delicious hot drinks, snacks, and even hearty meals, while reflecting on the day's adventures.

Good to Know

Ski Dubai is open from Monday to Friday, from 10:00 AM to midnight. On Saturdays and Sundays, it opens even earlier at 9:00 AM. Ticket prices start at around £50 per person, with many booking options available. For more information, visit www.skidxb.com.

How to Get There?

Mall of the Emirates

#17

4h

Relax on the Paradise Beach of **THE ISLAND**

More than a decade ago, the ambitious project to create the World Islands off the coast of Dubai began. The result is a collection of 300 islands that were intended to represent the continents of the world map.

The "The World" project faced numerous obstacles when it launched in 2003. Financial challenges and natural forces caused delays and changes to the appearance of the islands. Today, you can only vaguely recognize that the islands were meant to resemble the world map.

One island you can visit among the World Islands is Lebanon Island, known as "The Island". Just a 15-minute boat ride away, this idyllic archipelago offers an atmosphere of exclusivity where you can spend unforgettable hours. Experience the charm of a secluded paradise beach, surrounded by turquoise waters and lined with fine golden sand. On "The

The World Islands

Libanon Island (The Island)

Island", you'll find an oasis of absolute tranquility and relaxation with plenty of privacy. Sit back, enjoy the gentle sea breezes, and listen to the soothing sound of the waves. "The Island" is a true hidden gem, often giving the feeling that you have the entire place to yourself, as visitor numbers remain low depending on the season.

Time flies on "The Island". You can take advantage of the complimentary sun loungers to soak up the sun or dive into exciting sports activities like beach volleyball. The entrance fee also covers access to the sanitary facilities and towels. If you wish, you can also use canoes or stand-up paddles free of charge. Throughout the day, you can enjoy refreshing drinks at the bar.

Good to Know

The island is open daily from 10:00 AM to 6:00 PM. Admission to "The Island" costs approximately £65 for adults and £35 for children, with free entry for all children under 5 years old (more information available at www.theisland.ae). It's important to note that you must bring your passport for the trip, as you won't be allowed on the island without it.

How to Get There?

The boat ride to The Island takes about 15 minutes and departs from Jumeirah Fishing Harbour 1.

Bridge to the Island

A remarkable example of Dubai's pursuit of progress and innovation is the Museum of the Future – a truly impressive place that takes visitors on a journey into the world of tomorrow.

Particularly noteworthy are the intricate Arabic calligraphy designs that adorn the building. These masterful inscriptions not only serve as decoration but also function as windows. The museum rises to a height of about 78 meters and earned the honor of being listed among the 14 most beautiful museums in the world by National Geographic. Of the seven floors, five are dedicated to the main exhibition space. The sophisticated design of these rooms evokes the feeling of being on the set of a futuristic film.

The museum takes its visitors on an extraordinary journey to the year 2071. It presents various scenarios of how the future could be shaped in areas such as space exploration, ecosystems, bioengineering, health, wellness, and spirituality. A particularly inspiring part of the exhibition is

#18

4h

Experience the Future at THE MUSEUM OF THE FUTURE

called "New Moon", which explores the possibility of transforming the moon into a renewable energy source for the entire planet.

The first floor of the museum features the children's exhibition "Future Heroes", which is included in the admission price. It offers three main attractions – imagination, design, and building. Children have the opportunity to learn and play through activity-based experiences, promoting communication, cooperation, and

Interior of the Museum of the Future

Artistic Spiral Staircase

creativity. In a separate area, kids can tackle challenging missions together.

The museum isn't just focused on science and technology; it also places a strong emphasis on society. It asks the important question of how culture will be influenced by the integration of the latest technologies into daily life. The exhibits are designed to showcase the latest advancements in technology, science, sustainability, and design. Interactive displays, holograms, and virtual reality experiences allow visitors to immerse themselves in future scenarios and gain insight into how

our world might evolve. From artificial intelligence to renewable energy, the museum provides a comprehensive look at the potential paths the future could take.

Another central theme of the museum is climate change. Questions like "What technologies can help mitigate climate change?" and "What will life look like in 35 or even 50 years?" are explored here.

In addition to its permanent exhibitions, the museum also hosts temporary exhibitions that address the challenges and opportunities for the future of our planet. However, the museum is more than just a place for exhibits. It serves as a global hub for young talent, businesses, and technology enthusiasts. Here, they find not only opportunities for professional exchange but also expert support in realizing groundbreaking ideas. Dubai has been hosting the World Government Summit, a global event focused on futurism and emerging technologies, for many years. At the Museum of the Future, these crucial topics are made tangible and accessible to visitors. This innovative building provides a space where we can explore the future in new ways. Each year, about 150 countries participate in this event, which is a vibrant expression of our shared vision for a future-oriented world.

Good to Know

The museum is open daily from 10:00 AM to 9:30 PM. Admission is approximately £35 per person, and children under 4 years old have free entry (more information available at www.museumofthefuture.ae).

How to Get There?

Emirates Towers

#19

4h

Swimming at 210 Meters in the AURA SKYPOOL

Discover the breathtaking Aura Skypool in Dubai, a truly unique location situated around 210 meters high, featuring the world's highest infinity pool.

Experience pure relaxation while enjoying the stunning 360-degree panoramic views of the Palm Jumeirah, Dubai Marina, and Burj Khalifa. The Aura Skypool is located on the 50th floor of the Palm Tower and encircles the entire building. A visit to the Aura Skypool Lounge wouldn't be complete without indulging in the culinary delights offered here. The in-house restaurant features a variety of international dishes, crafted with fresh ingredients and presented beautifully. Enjoy delicious drinks like cocktails, mocktails, wine, and coffee, alongside a diverse menu of snacks, sushi, and sweet treats.

For your visit, all you need to bring are your swimwear and some money for food and drinks. Luxurious changing rooms are available for you to use, and a towel is included in the entrance fee. Additional towels or bathrobes can be rented for a fee. Lockers for valuables are also provided on-site.

The Aura Skypool Lounge in Dubai represents a place of grandeur, where luxury, relaxation, and world-class views come together in an impressive way. With unparalleled views of the city and a wide range of amenities, this lounge offers a chance to leave everyday life behind and immerse yourself in a world of elegance and tranquility.

Good to Know

The Aura Skypool is open from 6:00 AM until as late as 11:00 PM, though the hours vary depending on the day. There are several ticket options, allowing you to choose a special spot at the Skypool based on the time of day and the view you desire. A morning visit starts at around £55, while an afternoon visit begins at approximately £58. The "Full Day Ticket" for a full day at the pool costs around £110. For evening visits with a DJ, admission is about £47, but visitors must be at least 21 years old. Due to high demand, we recommend reserving tickets online in advance (more information at www.auraskypool.com). Entry is permitted for those aged 15 and up. However, 15- to 18-year-olds must be accompanied by an adult.

How to Get There?

The Palm Tower is connected to the Nakheel Mall on Palm Jumeirah. Rental cars, taxis, and the monorail offer various transportation options. We recommend taking a taxi for this activity.

#20

4h

California Meets
Dubai at the Unique
LA MER BEACH

4h Jumeirah

It's always a delightful experience to discover unexpected places during a vacation.

The California-inspired La Mer is one such destination, offering a unique atmosphere filled with sun, sea, and cultural surprises.

La Mer is divided into two areas – a northern and a southern beach section. Both bays are connected by a leisure center located on an artificial peninsula. This center houses a large waterpark called Laguna Waterpark, along with various boutiques and plenty of recreational opportunities.

The design of the entire district embraces a maritime theme, skillfully combining modern industrial design with driftwood, rusty anchors, barrels, and ropes. This approach not only raises awareness for sustainability but also creates a positive visual appeal for visitors. The wide, fine sandy beach, gently sloping turquoise waters with hardly any waves, and abundant sunshine all contribute to a particularly pleasant atmosphere.

Along the long beaches of La Mer, a charming promenade stretches out, lined with palm trees, numerous shops, and cafés. The attention to detail is clearly visible here. Surfboards, pirate ship motifs, beautifully crafted lamps, and playful animal sculptures can be found throughout the area. On the beach, visitors can rent sun loungers with umbrellas for relaxation. A special visual highlight at La Mer are the colorful beach houses, which contain showers and restrooms, adding to the vibrant atmosphere.

If you enjoy photography, La Mer offers plenty of interesting spots to capture. The artistic vibe of La Mer is unmistakable. Creative street art is scattered throughout the area, turning it into a colorful and lively environment. One standout is the popular photo spot featuring angel wings painted on a wall, reminiscent of the famous Instagram spot in Los Angeles. Don't miss the chance to discover some of the unique artworks and experience Dubai's creative side up close. Be sure to explore the hidden alleys and side paths to find lesser-known art pieces, often just as impressive as the more prominent ones.

La Mer transforms into a magical setting in the evening. The lighting of the restaurants, shops, and artworks creates a wonderfully romantic atmosphere. A stroll along the illuminated promenade after sunset is the perfect way to end a beach day at La Mer.

Good to Know

La Mer is a public beach and therefore open 24/7 (more information at www.lamerdubai.ae). Please note that swimming in the sea is prohibited after sunset in Dubai.

How to Get There?

Business Bay

From the Business Bay Metro Station, you can take bus line 9 to the Century Plaza 2 stop. From there, it's just a 10-minute walk to La Mer Beach.

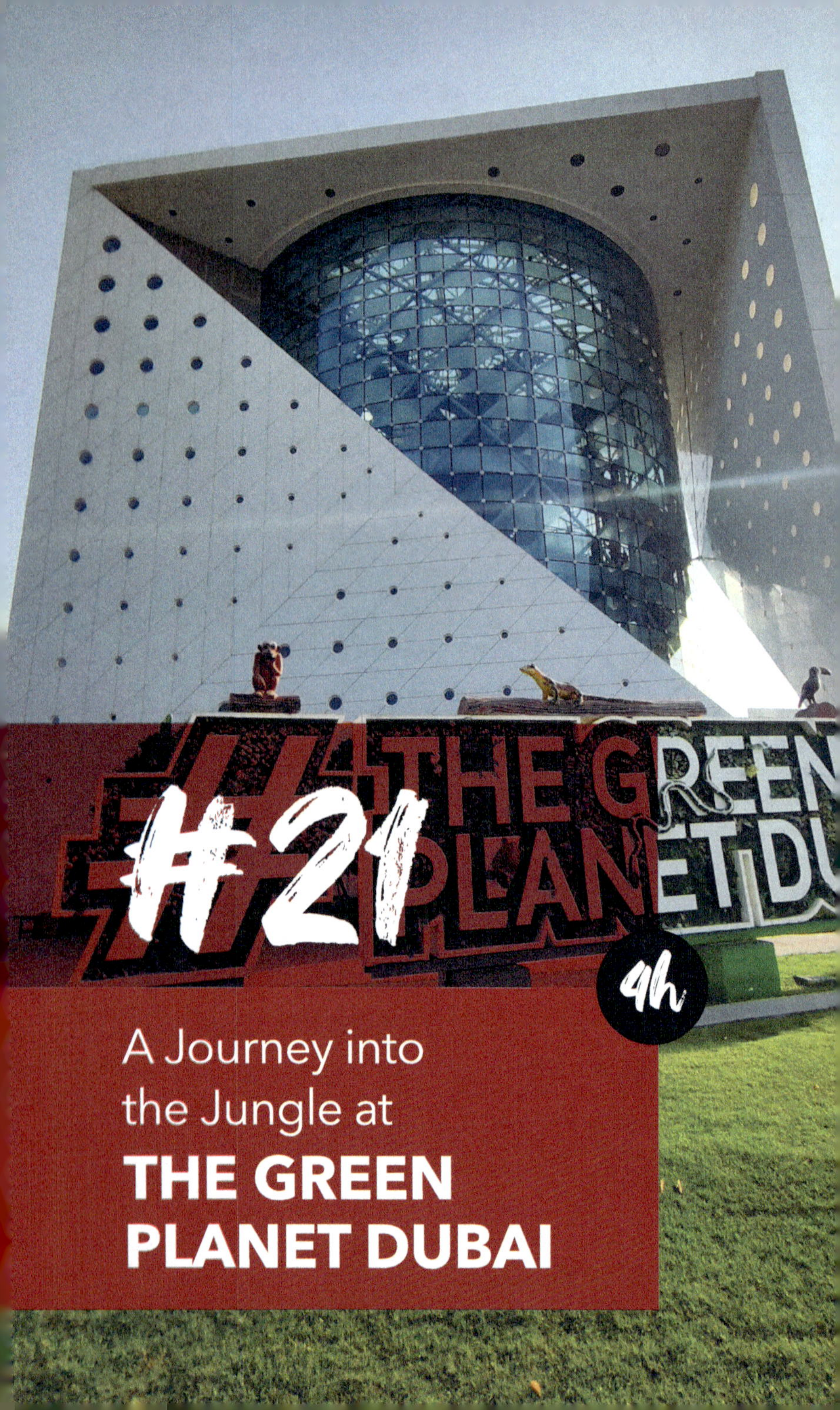

#21

4h

A Journey into the Jungle at

THE GREEN PLANET DUBAI

Is a tropical rainforest in the desert unthinkable? Not in Dubai! At "The Green Planet", you can actually explore an indoor jungle filled with exotic flora, fauna, and wild animals.

The building impresses with its sleek white exterior walls that enclose a glass cylinder. Inside The Green Planet, you'll find a complete tropical rainforest with controlled temperatures and humidity, just like in a real jungle. This unique ecosystem is home to more than 3,000 living creatures, including a variety of tropical plants, free-flying birds, fish, snakes, spiders, and frogs. The rainforest is built around an artificial tree that stands about 25 meters tall, with living plants attached to it. These plants are expected to fully cover the artificial tree within a few years. The development of the ecosystem, flora, and fauna in The Green Planet was carried out in close consultation with various experts in zoology and biology. This ensures that the rainforest becomes as close to a real one as possible, with plants and animals able to reproduce within the indoor environment.

The construction of The Green Planet was done in layers, corresponding to

The Green Planet Dubai

The Artificial Tree at the Heart of The Green Planet

the different environments found in a rainforest. Your discovery tour begins on the ground floor of the jungle. In the "Flooded Forest", you'll find aquariums with rays, turtles, and various fish to admire. After exploring the "Flooded Forest", you can ascend to the next level, where you can observe the rainforest up close from one of the narrow paths by the waterfall. You'll see tropical plants, lizards, and various species of frogs. A variety of insects also crawl along the ground, including the so-called "green ant", a subspecies of weaver ants. These small jungle dwellers build their nests by gluing leaves together.

Various spiders can also be found here, including the Goliath birdeater, the largest tarantula in the world. Numerous colorful birds soar through the air, including the largest species of toucan, the toco toucan. For the adventurous, the "Bat Cave" offers a mysterious encounter with bats. You can also spot a male and female sloth, along with many squirrel monkeys, as you continue your discovery tour through the jungle. While the animals in The Green Planet should not be touched, you might find a butterfly landing gently on your shoulder.

Take the elevator to the highest point of The Green Planet, where you'll enjoy a breathtaking panoramic view over the rainforest, complete with its waterfalls, plants, and animals, as the unique sounds of the jungle echo in the background.

A truly unique experience is camping in the rainforest, an activity offered by The Green Planet. Camping in the rainforest is available only on Fridays and Saturdays. Your adventurous camping journey begins with a hearty dinner and also includes a delicious breakfast at The Green Planet Café. One of the highlights is the nighttime tour through the rainforest, where you can observe all the nocturnal animals up close. The program is completed by feeding the animals and an exclusive behind-the-scenes tour, giving you a deeper insight into life in the rainforest.

For young nature enthusiasts, there's even a nature-themed movie or storytime that will captivate the whole family. And if you're wondering how you can freshen up during your stay, don't worry – there are restroom and shower facilities available to ensure your comfort.

The Green Planet offers an impressive experience that feels like a real tropical rainforest. The thoughtfully designed exhibit, with lush vegetation and exotic birdsong, creates a unique jungle atmosphere.

Good to Know

The Green Planet is open daily from 10:00 AM to 6:00 PM. A regular day ticket costs approximately £35 per person, while the special rainforest camping experience costs around £155 per person (more information at www.thegreenplanetdubai.com).

How to Get There?

Business Bay

Take the Metro to Business Bay Station, then hop on bus line 14 to the City Walk 2 stop. From there, it's about a 10-minute walk to The Green Planet.

#22

4h

Enjoy Beach Spa and Water Sports at **PALM WEST BEACH**

Palm West Beach, a stunning beach destination, is located at the lower end of the Palm Jumeirah island.

Though it shares the name "West Palm Beach" with its counterpart in Florida, United States, these two places are quite different. At Palm West Beach, you'll find a serene, idyllic coastline perfect for sun and sea lovers, along with various dining and nightlife options. Relax under palm trees and umbrellas, listening to the gentle sound of the sea, or treat yourself to a massage at the beach spa.

Over the years, Palm West Beach has steadily transformed. The area around the beach started as a modest setting but gradually developed into an enticing, contemporary retreat with exciting beach activities and upscale restaurants. At Palm West Beach, you can enjoy a variety of water sports such as kayaking, stand-up paddling, and jet skiing along the stunning coastline. The crystal-clear waters of the ocean also offer excellent opportunities for snorkeling and diving. Cycling, rollerblading, or jogging are also popular activities along the beach.

Experience some of the most exciting festivals and events held throughout the year at Palm West Beach. These include the high-end Dubai Food Festival, various yoga classes, the popular Palm West Beach Run (an annual 2.5k, 5k, or 10k marathon), and live DJ sets. In addition to these highlights, Palm West Beach also hosts the Beach Market, where you can enjoy a unique shopping experience at shops and market stalls offering handmade soaps, beachwear, accessories, and many other exquisite items.

A true visual delight awaits you in the evening when the promenade is beautifully illuminated by over 300 idyllic palm trees. Whether day or night, indulge in the culinary delights offered at the variety of restaurants along Palm West Beach. Be sure to try one of the best truffle risottos at "SĀN Beach" or enjoy an exceptionally delicious breakfast at "Jones the Grocer". Other highly recommended restaurants and venues at Palm West Beach include the "Surf Club", "February 30", and "Black Flamingo".

Good to Know

Palm West Beach also warmly welcomes dogs. Additionally, there is a large walking trail at the back of the beach, offering a perfect change of pace.

How to Get There?

Al Khail

You can take the Metro to Al Khail Station and then ride the Palm Jumeirah Monorail to Al Ittihad Park Station. From there, it's just a few minutes' walk to Palm West Beach. Alternatively, you can also arrive by taxi or rental car.

#23
4h
Panoramic Views and
Gourmet Dining at
PIER 7

In the heart of Dubai Marina stands Pier 7, a distinctive seven-story building that houses excellent gourmet restaurants on each floor.

Whether you're craving British pub fare or Peruvian specialties, the restaurants at Pier 7 offer a delectable selection of dishes from around the world. Conveniently located at Dubai Marina, Pier 7 enjoys a prime location. Thanks to its circular design and large terraces on each floor, visitors can enjoy panoramic views of the water and the vibrant district.

A chic restaurant with an Art Deco-inspired lounge awaits you on the top floor of Pier 7. Atelier M is the best place in Dubai to enjoy contemporary international cuisine. Gather with friends over stylish cocktails and look forward to a delicious meal on the rooftop terrace. The Atelier M menu features exquisite dishes, including some delightful chef specialties. The restaurant is also home to one of the best bars in Dubai Marina. Don't miss trying the truffle seafood gourmet pizza and the Black Onyx rib-eye.

The Asia Asia Restaurant & Lounge serves delicious Asian cuisine inspired by the ancient spice route. The restaurant is elegantly decorated with unique artifacts, while the lounges are themed after exotic destinations like Kyoto, Shanghai, Thailand, and Macau, each offering a distinct ambiance for guests. At Asia Asia, you can indulge your taste buds with a fusion of pan-Asian delicacies and the finest cocktails. This award-winning restaurant is one of the top dining destinations in the city and is famous for its popular sushi buffets in Dubai. Dishes like salmon carpaccio, maki, sashimi, and shrimp tempura are a true delight here.

Abd El Wahab is a traditional Lebanese restaurant in Pier 7, featuring oriental décor with brass ornaments and Damascus walls. Named after a street in Beirut, Abd El Wahab offers fresh and authentic Lebanese classics, including grilled dishes, mezze (traditional appetizers), and a variety of seafood specialties.

Scene Restaurant at Pier 7 is an excellent choice if you're looking for British favorites. This classic English pub-restaurant with rustic charm offers a cozy seating area and a terrace with stunning views of the Arabian Gulf and Dubai Marina. Here, you can indulge in hearty pies, steaks, and, of course, delicious fish and chips.

Cargo at Pier 7 serves the finest Asian cuisine with innovative cocktail selections. The menu at Cargo features a mix of Japanese, Thai, and Chinese favorites. You can enjoy everything from sushi and crispy chili beef to Thai green curry and Sichuan chicken. Pair your meal with a refreshing cocktail from the restaurant's bar menu.

For a cozy steak night, head to Mama Zonia. Located on the second floor, this restaurant serves Caribbean, Asian, and Peruvian cuisine. Designed to

Pier 7 at Dubai Marina

imitate the Amazon jungle in a chic urban setting, Mama Zonia offers bold tropical flavors, and their handcrafted cocktails complement the menu perfectly.

The modern Bedrock Sports Restaurant is a paradise for sports fans. Here, you can enjoy delicious dishes such as Wagyu steaks, fries, salads, and Italian pizzas while watching exciting live sports broadcasts on around 20 TV screens. Additionally, you can test your skills in a game of darts or try out the futuristic golf simulator at Bedrock Sports Restaurant.

Discover the variety and sophistication of the culinary offerings at Pier 7 and experience unforgettable gastronomic moments in the heart of Dubai.

Good to Know

The restaurants and lounges at Pier 7 are generally open daily, from early morning until late at night. However, prior reservations are highly recommended (more information at www.pier7.ae). Prices vary depending on the restaurant, but main courses typically range between £25 and £60.

How to Get There?

DMCC

#24

4h

Visit the World's Largest Ferris Wheel on **BLUEWATERS ISLAND**

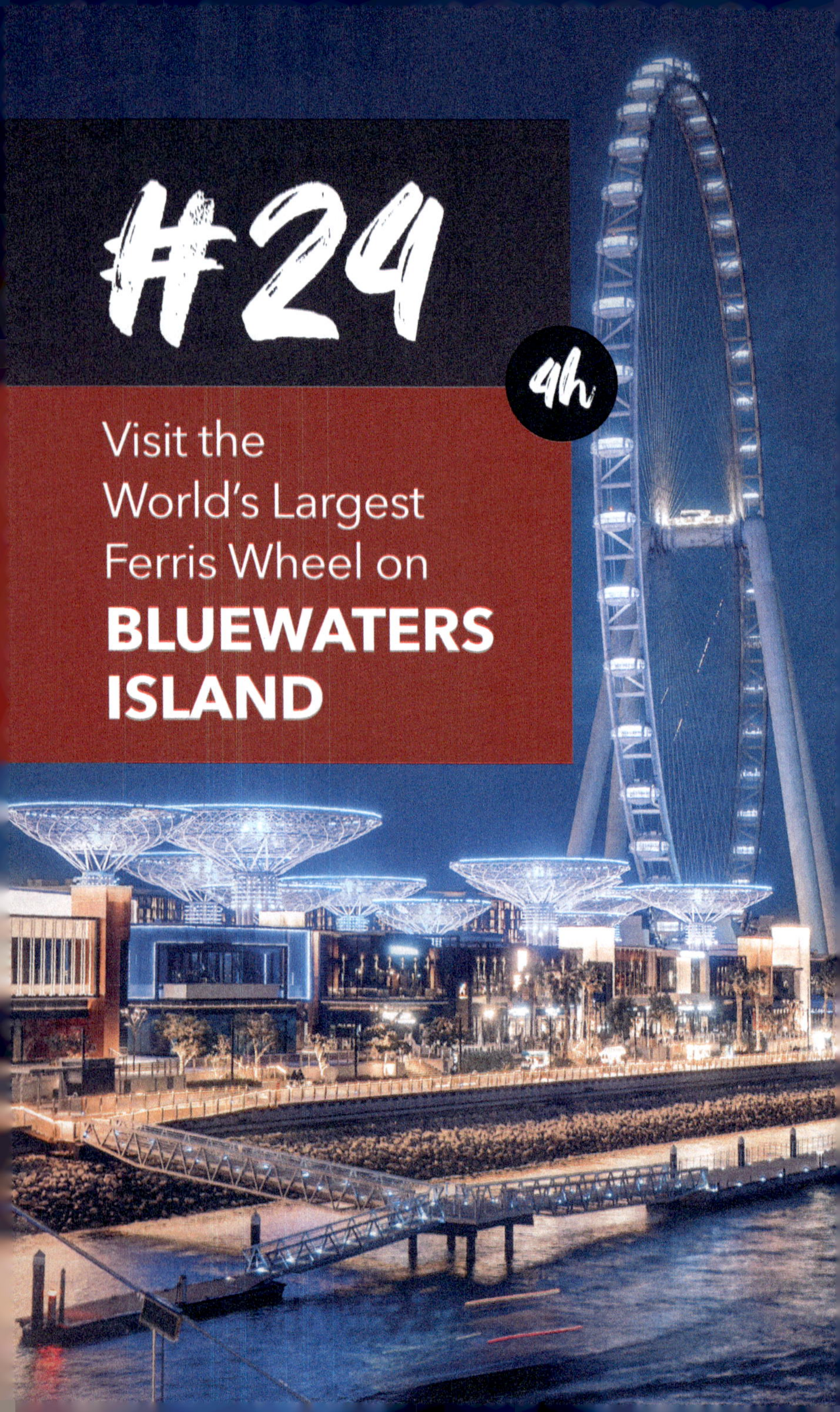

Bluewaters Island, just off Dubai's mainland, boasts a distinctive landmark – Ain Dubai, the world's largest Ferris wheel.

In addition to the Ferris wheel, the island offers an inviting blend of tranquility and urban excitement with luxury hotels, shopping, events, cultural attractions, and a charming promenade.

Ain Dubai, the world's largest Ferris wheel, officially opened on October 21, 2021. The first ride was celebrated with a spectacular fireworks display and a grand light show. From the air-conditioned cabins, guests can enjoy a panoramic view of the sea and the city's skyline. Additionally, the visitor capsules are equipped with bar lounges, and some are even designed to host dinners for an unforgettable dining experience.

In addition to the world's largest Ferris wheel, Bluewaters Island is proud to offer visitors another highly sought-after attraction. The prestigious Madame Tussauds wax museum has found its home in the Bluewaters Mall. This extraordinary wax museum showcases an impressive collection of 60 renowned figures from the worlds of film, music, fashion, politics, and sports. You'll also find a variety of wax figures featuring Bollywood celebrities and prominent stars from the Middle East.

Notable figures at the Dubai exhibit include British Queen Elizabeth II, famous actors like Tom Cruise and Audrey Hepburn, music stars such as Pharrell Williams and Lady Gaga, and celebrated athletes like Lionel Messi. Not only can you admire these popular wax figures up close, but you'll also find the perfect spot to pose for selfies with your favorite stars.

Around the Ain Dubai Ferris wheel on Bluewaters Island, a new lifestyle and shopping district called "The Wharf" has emerged. Gradually, over 100 shops, restaurants, and cafés will open in this area. The space surrounding Ain Dubai and "The Wharf" has been thoughtfully designed, offering visitors plenty of room for leisurely strolling and shopping. To enhance the festive atmosphere, food trucks and small entertainment stands are set up along the Ferris wheel plaza. Bluewaters Island also provides stunning views of Dubai's illuminated skyline at night.

Additionally, there are various activities for children, including small London-style double-decker buses and go-karts zipping along the promenade.

If you're looking to spend quality time with friends and family while enjoying great food and entertainment, "Brass Monkey" on Bluewaters Island is the perfect spot. This unique entertainment bar guarantees a pleasant experience for all visitors. Alongside a selection of tapas, salads, and delicious pizzas, the stylish gastropub serves refreshing cocktails as well

Bluewaters Island

as freshly brewed cappuccinos and other unique coffee variations. After your meal, you can indulge in various activities like billiards, bowling, or fun video games on retro arcade machines. Alternatively, guests can enjoy air hockey or foosball for some extra fun.

Another unique highlight awaits at "The Pods" on Bluewaters Island. Transparent cocoons not only ensure you dine in exclusive company but also shield you from sunlight while seated outdoors. A botanical-inspired decor enhances the relaxed outdoor atmosphere. The menu features pan-Asian dishes from Burma and Malaysia.

Charming courtyards, picturesque pedestrian zones around Ain Dubai, and scenic walkways along the waterfront invite visitors to leisurely stroll around Bluewaters Island. Additionally,

Cozy Cocoons at "The Pods" Restaurant

a 265-meter-long pedestrian bridge called "The Wharf Link" conveniently connects Bluewaters Island to the mainland coast. Bluewaters Island is a hub of fun and entertainment. Don't miss the live concerts, outdoor movie screenings, and other cultural events that regularly take place on the island.

How to Get There?

Jabal Ali

Take the Metro to Jabal Ali Station. From there, you can catch bus line F57 to the Bluewaters Island 1 stop.

#25

4h

DUBAI'S GOLF PARADISE

Swing Your Club in the Land of 1001 Nights

4h
Jumeirah

Golfing in Dubai

Dubai offers an impressive selection of golf courses set against the enchanting backdrop of 1001 Nights.

Golfing in Dubai is accessible to players of all skill levels, whether you're new to the sport or an experienced golfer. The city boasts some of the most prestigious golf courses in the world, renowned for their impeccable maintenance and exceptional service. Nearly all golf clubs provide equipment rentals, golf lessons, and professional shops to ensure golfers have everything they need. Non-golfers can also enjoy the fantastic amenities, including pools, fitness facilities, and dining options. With pleasant temperatures from September to May, Dubai provides the perfect climate for an extraordinary golfing adventure.

Dubai is home to three of the world's top 100 golf courses, which host major international tournaments. The dazzling Dubai skyline adds a remarkable touch to prestigious events like the Omega Dubai Desert Classic and the DP World Tour Championship. Renowned golfers such as Tiger Woods have graced these courses with their presence in the past.

There are also numerous hotels in Dubai designed for golf vacations. Two prime examples of luxury golf hotels near the prestigious 18-hole championship course at Dubai Creek Golf Club are the InterContinental Festival City and the Park Hyatt Dubai.

If you're interested in casual golfing, we highly recommend a visit to Topgolf Dubai at the Emirates Golf Club. This unique facility seamlessly blends golf with entertainment and exquisite dining options. Guests can enjoy a relaxed round of golf while scoring points in a comfortable setting. Additionally, Topgolf Dubai is an ideal venue for special occasions such as birthday celebrations.

Good to Know

Most golf courses in Dubai are open year-round. Green fees range from £40 to £210 per player, depending on the course (more information on all golf courses and prices can be found at www.bydubaigolf.com).

How to Get There?

Jabal Ali

Most courses are easily accessible by metro, taxi, or rental car. If you're visiting Topgolf Dubai, take the metro to Jabal Ali Station, and from there, it's about a 10-minute walk to the golf facility.

#26

4h

Relax Away from the Crowds at the **HIDDEN SECRET BEACH**

Dubai's Al Sufouh Beach, often referred to as Secret Beach or Black Palace Beach, remains one of the city's best-kept secrets.

This secluded stretch of coastline spans an impressive 2,5 km and is conveniently located near the iconic Palm Jumeirah, yet its presence is cleverly concealed by a vibrant palm oasis. Visitors can escape the city's modern hustle and enjoy a serene setting of soft white sand and the calm waters of the Arabian Gulf, while taking in a breathtaking sunset over the Arabian horizon. The views of Palm Jumeirah, the Burj Al Arab, and Dubai's skyline are simply stunning.

Al Sufouh Beach, open year-round, has limited facilities, so it's advisable to bring your own food and water. Visitors can enjoy various activities at this hidden gem, including unique photo sessions with the Burj Al Arab in the background, relaxing picnics with good company, a refreshing swim in the warm waters of the Arabian Gulf, and unforgettable sunset experiences.

Good to Know

The beach is open 24 hours daily and can be visited free of charge.

How to Get There?

Bus line 8 takes you to the Dubai College 2 stop, from which it's about a 15-minute walk to the beach. Alternatively, you can take a taxi directly to Al Sufouh 1.

Paradise at "Secret Beach" with the Burj Al Arab in the Distance

#27

4h

YACHT CRUISES

in Dubai Marina

Step aboard and enjoy an unforgettable time – experience the variety of yacht cruises in Dubai Marina.

Discover the beauty of the city from the water as you pass iconic landmarks like Atlantis The Palm, Burj Al Arab, The World Islands, and the legendary Bluewaters Island. These sightseeing yacht cruises offer a unique perspective on Dubai's inspiring skyline. The tours last about 2-4 hours, giving you the chance to see the breathtaking sights from a whole new angle.

For an exclusive experience, we recommend private yacht cruises. Fulfill your dream of hosting your own yacht party. Whether it's a romantic getaway for two or a celebration with friends, a wide selection of yachts is available to suit your needs. Treat yourself to a customized sunset cruise for an even more special experience. Experienced captains and crew will accompany you on your journey, ensuring safety and comfort.

For a top-tier culinary experience, the yacht brunch & dinner cruises are highly recommended. Indulge in a luxurious dining experience on a larger yacht, complete with a variety of buffets or live cooking stations. Enjoy the tranquility of the Arabian Gulf and the entertainment program during this 2-hour tour.

If you enjoy fishing, then fishing trips in Dubai Marina are perfect for you. These tours typically last 4-5 hours and give you the opportunity to show off your fishing skills and grill your catch right on board.

Before booking your yacht trip, be sure to keep a few important rules in mind. Yacht rentals in Dubai Marina are charged by the hour, so plan your event's timing carefully. You'll be informed of the exact boarding time and location when you book. Dress comfortably, and consider bringing a light jacket if you're taking a night tour, as it can get a bit chilly. If you're prone to seasickness, it's advisable to bring medication to ensure you can fully enjoy the experience.

Good to Know

For bookings, we recommend the operator Xclusive Yachts. The company has been in business for over 15 years, with around 70 yachts and boats and more than 35 awards to its name. You can book a variety of yacht excursions directly online at www.xclusiveyachts.com. For a private yacht, you'll pay around £410 for 3 hours. A Sunset and Dinner Cruise with dinner costs approximately £60 for adults and around £35 for children (children under 3 are free).

How to Get There?

DMCC

#28

4h

Ride the Waves and Winds at Dubai's KITE BEACH

Dive into the crystal-clear waters and experience the thrill of kitesurfing at Kite Beach.

Don't worry if you're a beginner – the Kitesurf School Dubai offers professional lessons for newcomers, ensuring you feel safe and confident on the board. This spot is perfect for kitesurfing enthusiasts, with steady sea breezes and shallow waters providing the ideal conditions to explore the world of kitesurfing.

Guided by qualified instructors, you will learn the basics of equipment, safety, wind mechanics, and kitesurfing techniques. These lessons are designed to give you the confidence and skills necessary to venture out onto

4h Jumeirah

Kite Beach

Kitesurfer

the water. Before starting your kitesurfing adventure, you'll get familiar with the equipment. Safety comes first – you'll be provided with a wetsuit, life jacket, and a kiteboard specifically designed for beginners. Using the kite, or "sail", you'll harness the wind to glide from the beach into the vast expanse of the Gulf.

Once you've mastered the basics on land, it's time to transfer those skills to the water. Under the guidance of your experienced instructor, you'll first practice kite handling in shallow waters. Feeling the pull of the kite in your hands is an exhilarating experience. As you gain confidence, you'll eventually hop on the board, soaring across the water with the kite floating above you.

Your first successful rise onto the kiteboard brings a feeling of freedom that's hard to describe. You glide across the water, powered by the wind and guided by your developing skills. With each attempt, you refine your technique and balance, fully embracing the thrill of kitesurfing.

Kite Beach offers more than just an adrenaline-pumping kitesurfing experience – it also provides a laid-back, beachy atmosphere. After your session, relax on the sun loungers, enjoy refreshing drinks at the nearby cafés, and soak in the vibrant energy of this watersport paradise.

There are plenty of other activities to enjoy at Kite Beach as well. Watch the pros pull off daring tricks at the XDubai Skatepark on their skateboards, or play a game of beach volleyball while listening to the sound of the waves in the background. If you're in the mood for relaxation, the beach library offers a selection of books in both English and Arabic that you can enjoy for free. Just grab a book, find a cozy spot in the shade, and immerse yourself in captivating stories.

Good to Know

The beach is free to access and is open daily from 10:00 AM to 10:00 PM. The cost for kitesurfing varies depending on the duration, with prices starting at around £85 per hour (for more information, visit www.kitesurf.ae).

How to Get There?

Dubai Internet City

To get there, take the metro to Dubai Internet City Station, and from there, hop on Bus 88 to the Manara, Enoc 2 stop.

#29

Discover Oriental Charm in MADINAT JUMEIRAH

Madinat Jumeirah is not just a collection of luxury hotels, but rather a magical setting that will make your heart race.

As soon as you enter the complex, it feels like stepping into an oriental fairytale brought to life. The architectural design evokes bygone eras, with an incredible attention to detail visible in every corner. Madinat Jumeirah is a haven for those seeking relaxation. The luxurious hotels boast world-class facilities, including exclusive spas, private beaches, and pools, all designed to offer a serene escape. Treat yourself to a wide range of wellness treatments, from

8h Jumeirah

Abra ride along the waterways in Madinat Jumeirah

traditional Arabian techniques to modern approaches. Madinat Jumeirah spans around 3 km of beautiful waterways, surrounded by lush gardens, creating a perfect setting for visitors. This idyllic area consists of impressive hotels, all interconnected by turquoise waterways.

Visit the Madinat Souk, a charming Arabian bazaar with narrow alleyways and shops offering exquisite treasures and authentic souvenirs. Here, you'll be captivated by the variety of goods as you explore and discover delightful finds. The inviting restaurants tempt with culinary delights from around the world, while traditional cafés offer a serene break. Indulge your palate with delicious dishes and refreshing drinks as you watch the vibrant activity in the souk.

The stunning private beach at Madinat Jumeirah is an oasis of relaxation, offering a breathtaking view of the

Colorful lights in a shopping alley

Burj Al Arab. Enjoy the gentle waves of the Persian Gulf and let your gaze wander over the sparkling waters.

Within Madinat Jumeirah, you have the chance to explore the stunning waterways aboard traditional Abra boats. These wooden boats take you on peaceful and relaxing routes through the resort, passing elegant villas, lush gardens, and unique spots.

In addition to the numerous attractions, Madinat Jumeirah also offers a rich entertainment program. Visit the Madinat Theatre, one of Dubai's premier venues, and enjoy a variety of performances, including plays, concerts, and musicals. The Theatre of Digital Art Dubai showcases works by artists like Claude Monet and Wassily Kandinsky. This unique theater offers art lovers throughout the UAE the opportunity to experience masterpieces by some of the world's most renowned artists through digital shows,

Sunset at
Madinat Jumeirah

accompanied by impressive music, visual effects, and surround sound.

A day in Madinat Jumeirah is not just a journey into the past, but also an exploration of Dubai's beauty and diversity. In addition to world-class restaurants and cafés, you can also enjoy the vibrant nightlife, ending your evening in one of the bars or clubs. Pai Thai, one of the most popular Thai restaurants, is located within Madinat Jumeirah and can only be accessed via Abra boat across the Souk Madinat waterways. Enjoy a relaxing dinner at Pai Thai with a direct view of the peaceful Madinat Jumeirah canals.

To make the most of your visit, it's best to plan a little extra time to fully appreciate the charm and variety Madinat Jumeirah has to offer. There's so much to discover and experience that a single day may hardly be enough.

Good to Know

Entrance to the Madinat Jumeirah complex is free. However, if you want access to the private beach, a day pass costs approximately £65 during weekdays and around £80 on weekends. Abra rides are available starting from £8 to £10, depending on the tour. If you're staying at one of the Madinat Jumeirah hotels, you can enjoy complimentary access to the private beach and free Abra rides within the complex.

How to Get There?

Mashreq Metro Station

Madinat Jumeirah is centrally located in Dubai and easily accessible by taxi or metro (Mashreq Metro Station). From the Mashreq Metro Station, you can take bus line 88 or 81 to the Madinat Jumeirah 2 (88) or Dubai Police Academy 2 (81) stops.

#30

8h

Swim with Dolphins at AQUAVENTURE WATERPARK

Nestled on the man-made island of The Palm Jumeirah, Aquaventure Waterpark offers a stunning setting for thrilling adventures.

With an impressive array of waterslides and a variety of pools, Aquaventure is the perfect place to immerse yourself in refreshing fun and leave the daily grind behind.

Daredevil visitors can plunge into waterslides like the famous "Leap of Faith", where you drop vertically into the depths and then glide through a lagoon full of sharks and rays – a truly adrenaline-filled experience! For those who prefer a more relaxed pace, the "Lazy River" offers a gentle way to float on an inner tube through a serene water landscape. The leisurely river ride connects the slides of the "Tower of Poseidon" and the "Tower of Neptune" – the two main hubs for adventure and unlimited fun at the waterpark. A ride on the 2,3 km river adventure attraction, which winds around the entire tropical water landscape of Aquaventure, allows you to float gently for an impressive 45 minutes of relaxation. For those who want to take a break afterward,

The Famous "Leap of Faith" Waterslide

Aquaventure Waterpark

Swimming with Dolphins at Aquaventure Waterpark

the 500-meter long white sand beach of the waterpark offers the perfect retreat.

The encounters with dolphins at Dolphin Bay are truly unique experiences not to be missed. Dolphin Bay is a specially designed paradise that allows visitors to interact with dolphins in a safe and controlled environment. Before diving into the world of dolphins, you'll receive a detailed briefing from experienced handlers. These experts will not only teach you how to interact safely with the dolphins but also share valuable insights about their anatomy, behavior, and ecological importance. Safety is a top priority here, so strict rules and guidelines are in place to ensure that both guests and dolphins are protected. During the swimming experience, you'll have the opportunity to be side by side with the dolphins, touch them, pet them, and even swim with them. The dolphins are known for their friendliness and curiosity, leading to unforgettable moments. Qualified trainers accompany you throughout the experience, ensuring you have a rewarding and enjoyable time.

Good to Know

The water park is open daily from 10:00 AM to 5:30 PM. Prices range from approximately £80 to £160, depending on the package chosen. Included in the price are wetsuits, towels, lockers, complimentary juices after swimming with the dolphins, and most importantly, free access to the entire Aquaventure Waterpark on the same day (a regular day pass alone costs around £65 or about £75 if you also add access to "The Lost Chambers Aquarium"). Tickets can be easily reserved online at www.atlantis.com.

How to Get There?

Aquaventure Waterpark

We recommend traveling by taxi or rental car to Atlantis The Palm Hotel. Alternatively, you can take the monorail to the Aquaventure Waterpark station.

#31

2h

Cross the Dubai Creek in a **TRADITIONAL ABRA**

Explore Dubai the traditional way with a relaxing Abra ride along the Dubai Creek.

These hand-crafted wooden boats, available in various sizes, continue to serve as an essential mode of transportation across the historic river. Once a bustling hub of trade, the Creek was the starting point for Dubai's rise to a modern metropolis. Friendly Abra drivers wait by the shore, ready to take you on an unforgettable tour. The ride typically lasts between 30 and 60 minutes, depending on the route. Simply head to the Creek's shore, where drivers are always available for a ride. Haggling over the price is part of the experience, but a fair rate for an hour-long tour is usually around £25.

Once you're on the water, stunning photo opportunities along the Creek unfold. For travelers familiar with Dubai, traditional Abras are a popular and affordable way to cross from one side to the other. For just 1 Dirham (around £0.20), you can travel between stops like Deira Old Souk Abra Station and Bur Dubai Abra Station.

Abras aren't just a means of transportation; they are a living testament to Dubai's past. Around 150 of these boats still operate today, transporting nearly 100,000 people daily. The drivers, often from Pakistan, India, or Iran, may not speak much English, but communication is never an issue. For those seeking an air-conditioned option, the modern Dubai Waterbus is also available.

It's an unmistakable feeling to experience the warm breeze on an Abra and take in the essence of old Dubai. The ride offers a unique opportunity to enjoy Dubai's beauty from the water while observing the everyday life of locals.

Good to Know

Abra rides operate throughout the day with no fixed schedules, and departure times vary depending on passenger demand. A one-hour private Abra tour typically costs around £25 per person.

How to Get There?

Creek

The Abra stations are located at various points along the Creek, such as the Deira Old Souk Abra Station and the Dubai Old Souk Abra Station.

#32

2h

Discover Impressive Perspectives at the **DUBAI FRAME**

Since its opening on January 1, 2018, the rectangular Dubai Frame has proudly risen in Dubai's stunning skyline and has become one of the city's most impressive landmarks.

Standing 150 meters high and 93 meters wide, it boasts an unusual building design. Its strategic location between the old town and modern districts beautifully illustrates Dubai's successful blend of tradition and modernity.

The unmissable Dubai Frame is located in Zabeel Park. Upon closer inspection, a charming environment unfolds, with food trucks offering delicious snacks and freshly pressed juices, inviting visitors to linger. Green spaces with palm trees, fountains, and seating areas provide perfect photo opportunities in the plaza.

The tour through the Dubai Frame begins after a short wait in line. The Old Dubai Gallery is located in the mezzanine of the Dubai Frame. The exhibition showcases Dubai's humble beginnings as a Bedouin fishing village. It offers visitors an exciting journey through the history of Dubai, using historical exhibits and audiovisual presentations. The museum tells the story of the city's origins and illustrates its development into today's modern metropolis.

An absolute highlight is the ride in the glass panorama elevator, which takes visitors up to the connecting bridge in just 75 seconds, spanning

48 floors. From the top, a breathtaking 360-degree view of the entire metropolis unfolds. Through the large window fronts, you can see both the old town with the Dubai Creek and the skyline with the famous Burj Khalifa.

A special thrill awaits you on the connecting bridge. The glass floor offers a dizzying view straight down to the ground. Interactive touch displays also provide interesting information about the city's most significant landmarks.

On the way down, the mezzanine level on the other side of the Dubai Frame features the Future Dubai Gallery. This gallery takes visitors on a journey through time with stunning projections, creating the impression of a high-speed time machine transporting them into the Dubai of 2050. With special effects, it feels like a futuristic adventure. The entire tour lasts about 20 minutes, but you can stay longer on the platform. The Dubai Frame is not only a thrilling experience for adults but also an exciting adventure for children, sure to leave them with glowing eyes.

Good to Know

The Dubai Frame is open daily from 9:00 AM to 9:00 PM. Admission is approximately £10 for adults and about £4 for children. Children under the age of 3 can enter for free. Tickets can be booked online at www.dubaiframe.ae.

How to Get There?

Max

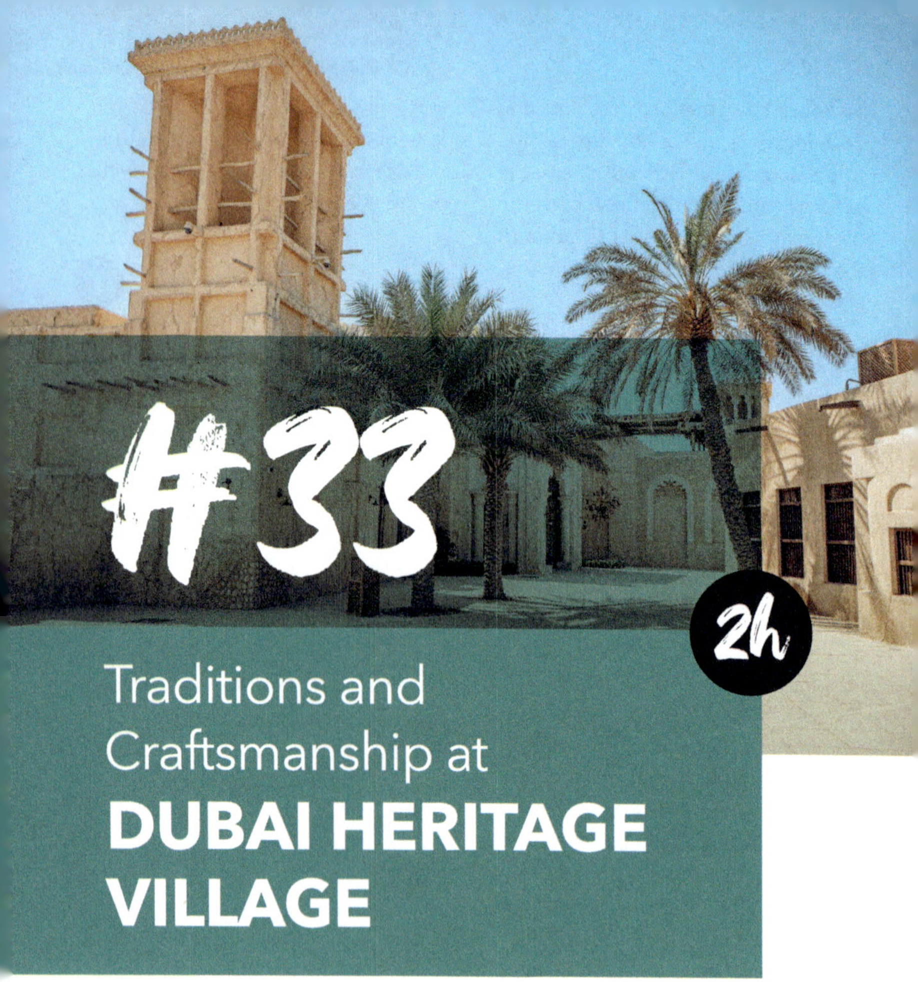

#33

2h

Traditions and Craftsmanship at **DUBAI HERITAGE VILLAGE**

Discover the Dubai Heritage Village, also known as the Al Shindagha Historic District, located near the mouth of the Creek in the Al Shindagha neighborhood.

Explore Dubai's ancient traditions and embark on a journey into the past.

The first stop in the Heritage Village is the local artisans who specialize in weaving baskets, rugs, and other handicrafts. This art of weaving has been passed down through generations by their ancestors. Beautiful products are also available here as souvenirs for the family. Another popular craft in the Heritage Village is pottery. You'll find many local artisans who are experts in pottery-making. Additionally, you can join fun workshops, especially great for families. Children enjoy learning and shaping clay. In the village, you can also see horses, camels, and ducks around a small pond.

Locals take care of these animals, and visitors can feed them and even enjoy horse or camel rides.

An exciting activity in the Heritage Village is exploring the pearl diving industry. This 7,000-year-old industry has been a long-standing tradition in Dubai and is still alive in certain parts of the Heritage Village. The diving expedition, consisting of around 60 people, including the captain and crew, embarks on a month-long search for precious stones.

At the local authentic cultural center in the Heritage and Diving Village, you can purchase unique handmade products like clothing, baskets, pots, and pearl jewelry. These souvenirs help support the local economy.

Culinary delights are also abundant in the Heritage Village. Try the popular dish hummus, made from chickpeas, garlic, and olive oil, served with local bread. Authentic shawarma, a traditional Arabic meat dish with lamb or chicken and various toppings, is also highly recommended. For something different, you can enjoy Iranian tea served with honey and lemon. The local restaurants and cafés offer delicious seafood dishes as well. Additionally, there are stands selling seafood, snacks, and beverages.

The Heritage Village Dubai, opened in 1997, offers an authentic glimpse into life in the past. The restored stone houses and tents transport you back in time, showcasing the old farming methods and craftsmanship once used by the people of this region. The Heritage Village is the perfect place to purchase a traditional Arabic souvenir and is also a popular destination for Dubai residents. Regular events featuring Arabic music and folk dances add a lively atmosphere to the area. Visiting the Heritage Village is especially enjoyable in the evening, with a picturesque view of Dubai's illuminated skyline.

Good to Know

The Dubai Heritage Village is open daily from 8:00 AM to 8:00 PM, and on Fridays and Saturdays from 4:00 PM to 10:00 PM. Admission is free.

How to Get There?

Al Ghubaiba

Bastakiya

2h Bur Dubai

#34

2h

BASTAKIYA
The Artist District by Dubai Creek

Step into the charming Bastakiya, also known as Al Fahidi Historical District, the artistic heart of Dubai.

This historic neighborhood, stretching along Dubai Creek, is a remarkable testament to the past and is now a protected heritage site. Upon entering this enchanting quarter, you are transported into a world of traditional Arab heritage.

Bastakiya is home to Al Fahidi Fort, one of Dubai's oldest buildings, proudly showcasing its history. Originally inhabited by wealthy Iranian settlers, the neighborhood enchants visitors today with its restored alleyways and distinctive wind towers, which once acted as "natural fans" to cool the heat. The houses in the Al Fahidi District are made of stone, gypsum, shells, limestone, sandalwood, and palm wood, offering a vivid impression of life in Dubai before the oil boom. Interestingly, the area faced demolition plans in the 1990s, but a prominent advocate, Prince Charles of England, successfully campaigned to preserve it.

As a true artistic district, Bastakiya is filled with galleries displaying works by talented local and international artists. Art lovers will be captivated by the variety and creative spirit of this

Idyllic Alley
in Bastakiya

place. Don't miss the cultural center, which regularly hosts inspiring exhibitions and events. The Sikka Art and Design Festival, part of the Dubai Art Season, showcases modern street art murals and abstract sculptures in the quarter. As you stroll through Bastakiya, you'll discover charming cafes, craft shops, galleries, and museums, many of which can be visited for free or with minimal admission fees.

Another exciting highlight is attending a cultural lunch at the Sheikh Mohammed Centre for Cultural Understanding (SMCCU). Here, you'll have the opportunity to learn about the culture, religion, and traditions of the United Arab Emirates while enjoying delicious food and engaging in open dialogue with locals. The SMCCU offers humorous insights into Emirati culture and also provides guided tours around Dubai Creek.

For a culinary break, we recommend the Arabian Tea House, offering classic Arabic meals in an authentic setting. Nearby, The Majlis Gallery showcases modern works by international artists in a charming courtyard.

The Bastakiya Quarter is located on the Bur Dubai side of the Dubai Creek and is easily accessible. Be sure to also visit the Dubai Museum in the nearby Al Fahidi Fort to learn more about the rich history of this vibrant metropolis.

Good to Know

Galleries are generally open from 10:00 AM to 6:00 PM, while cafés and restaurants typically operate from 7:00 AM to 10:00 PM. The cultural lunch at the SMCCU is available from Monday to Thursday at 1:00 PM. Admission is usually free, although some galleries and cultural events may charge an entrance fee. The cultural lunch at the SMCCU costs around £32 per person, with children aged 7 to 12 paying half the price, and children under 7 attending for free. There are also dinner and brunch options available (for more information, visit www.cultures.ae/program).

How to Get There?

Sharaf DG

Learn About the Journey of Coffee in the Middle East at the **DUBAI COFFEE MUSEUM**

The Dubai Coffee Museum is the perfect place to discover the history of coffee and its journey into the Middle East.

At the museum, you can explore a variety of coffee types and experience different coffee cultures such as Arabic, Ethiopian, and Egyptian. The museum offers insights into the entire process, from bean selection to roasting and the unique brewing methods of each culture.

The Coffee Museum tells the legend of Kaldi, a shepherd who is said to have discovered the first coffee bean, as well as the long journey of coffee from the Ethiopian mountains to the Middle East. Visitors can browse through old cups and utensils once used for coffee making and brewing, with antique exhibits showcasing tools from times past.

The main hall of the museum highlights global coffee production and consumption. On the first floor, a selection of coffee books dating back to the 18th century from the owner's personal collection offers coffee enthusiasts a deeper insight into the beloved drink. In addition, audiovisual guides provide an informative perspective. There's also a special area for children, ensuring fun and entertainment for the little ones.

In the museum shop of the Dubai Coffee Museum, you can find ideal souvenirs and gifts. Here, you'll discover exquisite coffee beans to enjoy, various roasting technique books, latte art pens, and barista accessories. Of course, you can also enjoy freshly brewed coffee and delicious snacks during your visit.

Good to Know

The museum is open from Saturday to Thursday, from 9:00 AM to 5:00 PM, and is closed on Fridays. Admission is currently free (there was a time when a small fee was charged).

How to Get There?

Sharaf DG

Dubai Coffee Museum

#36

4h

Attend a Traditional Emirati **COOKING CLASS**

Participants at Al Khayma Heritage House can enjoy a hands-on experience as they learn to cook traditional Emirati dishes, guided by expert chefs.

These cooking classes offer a unique opportunity to dive into the culinary culture of the United Arab Emirates, exploring local ingredients, techniques, and the stories behind the dishes.

The cooking classes at Al Khayma Heritage House offer various options, including 1.5-hour breakfast courses, 2-hour courses on preparing Machboos (a traditional rice and chicken dish), and 3-hour courses covering the preparation of Machboos, Regag bread (a thin, crispy bread), and Lokma (a traditional dessert). Participants have the opportunity to learn from skilled chefs and acquire hands-on skills to recreate these authentic dishes at home.

These cooking classes provide not only a culinary experience but also a cultural learning journey. During the courses, participants gain insights into the history and significance of each dish within Emirati culture, allowing them to appreciate both the flavors and the stories behind the meals they prepare.

The cooking classes at Al Khayma Heritage House are popular among tourists eager to delve deeper into the culture and cuisine of the Emirates. These interactive and enjoyable classes offer a unique way to experience and understand the region's heritage through food.

Good to Know

The classes are held daily. The breakfast course begins at 7:00 AM, the lunch course at 2:00 PM, and the dinner course at 7:00 PM. The dinner class costs around £75, the lunch class is approximately £60, and the breakfast class is about £35 per person (more information available at www.alkhayma.com).

How to Get There?

Sharaf DG

#37

2h

Discover the Stories of Strong Women **AT THE WOMEN'S MUSEUM**

The Women's Museum, also known as the Bait Al Banat Women's Museum, is a cultural initiative unique to the Arab world and the Gulf region.

Founded by Emirati woman Professor Rafia Ghubash, the museum aims to preserve the history of women in the United Arab Emirates and challenge stereotypes. It provides a space to explore and celebrate the lives of women from the UAE. Located in the Deira district, the museum is dedicated to showcasing women's contributions in various aspects of life, including social, cultural, educational, and economic fields.

Visiting the Women's Museum offers an enriching journey through time, highlighting the lives and achievements of Emirati women in science, culture, business, and art.

The museum also serves as a national archive and documentation center, dedicated to all aspects of women's lives in the UAE. Many visitors are impressed by the aesthetic design of the building. The exhibitions are well-curated, providing an insightful look into various aspects of women's lives and contributions in the UAE. These exhibits not only share historical knowledge but also tell inspiring stories of strong and influential Emirati women.

The Women's Museum strives to raise awareness of the role of women in society and highlight their contributions across various fields. It showcases a wide range of historical and cultural exhibits that depict the heritage and history of women in the UAE.

Good to Know

The entrance fee is approximately £4. The museum is open from Saturday to Thursday, from 10:00 AM to 5:30 PM (for more information, visit www.womenmuseum-uae.com).

How to Get There?

Al Ras

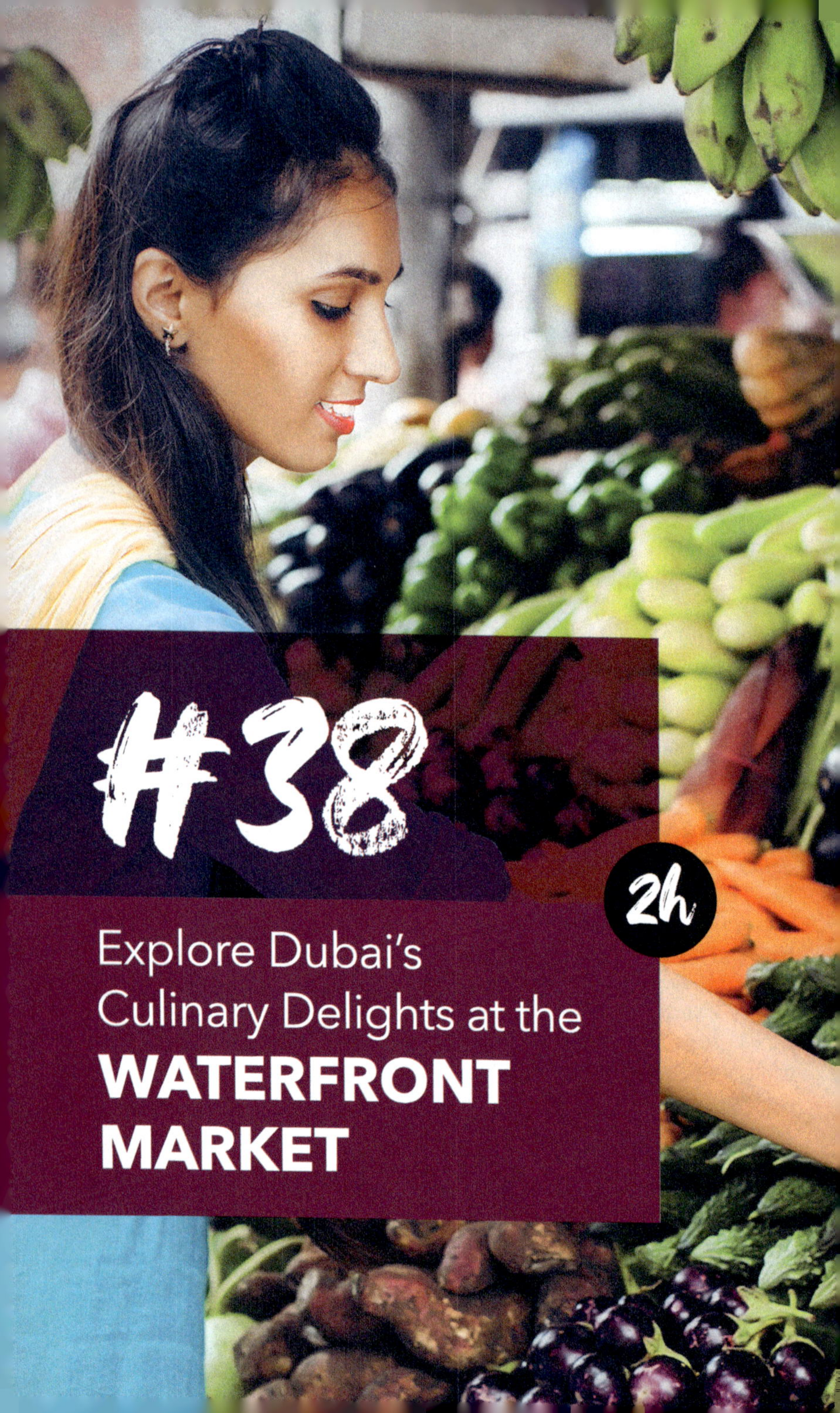

#38

2h

Explore Dubai's Culinary Delights at the WATERFRONT MARKET

Pier at the Waterfront Market

The Waterfront Market is a popular destination for those seeking high-quality fresh produce.

Over time, the market has become a significant part of Dubai's food culture, blending local traditions with international influences and offering a variety of experiences for both locals and visitors.

Fresh fruits and vegetables are offered by over 150 vendors, including local, regional, and imported products. The market is as diverse as the various nationalities and ethnic groups it serves. You'll find seasonal delicacies sourced directly from farms in the UAE.

For seafood lovers, the market is a must-visit. More than 500 vendors present over 350 seasonal varieties from the region and beyond. Live, fresh, and dried seafood options are available, and a special section allows you to have your selection prepared to your liking.

In the meat and poultry market, you'll be spoiled for choice. Over 80 dedicated butchers offer a wide variety of meats, including beef, goat, chicken, lamb, and camel. All products

are sourced from local, regional, and international farms. Here, hygiene and food safety are given the utmost priority.

The spice and dry goods market zone takes you into a sensory wonderland. With vibrant spices, aromatic products, and the bustling atmosphere of a traditional Arabic souk, this area features over 60 shops offering a wide range of products, including nuts, sweets, spices, rice, and more. You can purchase by the piece, kilo, or in bulk.

A culinary experience awaits you with a diverse selection of restaurants and cafés at reasonable prices. Whether you prefer cozy seating or take-away options, there's something for everyone. The promenade offers stunning views of the Deira Corniche and the Deira Islands. You can also buy fresh fish and seafood and have it prepared by one of the waterfront restaurants to enjoy.

The Waterfront Market is a family-friendly destination with play areas for kids, activities along the promenade, and spaces for relaxed gatherings. The market impresses with a vast array of fresh produce from around the world. Chat with the vendors to find the best ingredients for BBQs or authentic meals. We recommend visiting the market in the early morning to get the freshest products.

Good to Know

Most markets at the Waterfront Market are open from early morning until midnight (more information can be found at www.waterfrontmarket.ae).

How to Get There?

Union

You can take the metro to Union Station. From there, you can catch one of the many bus connections, such as line C28 from Memorial Plaza to Hamriya, Masjid 1. Afterward, it's just a short walk to the Waterfront Market. Alternatively, you can also take a taxi, with many taxi stands available on-site at the Waterfront Market.

#39

2h

Discover Serenity at the **MOSQUE OF LIGHT**

The Gargash Mosque, also known as the "Mosque of Light", is an extraordinary landmark and place of worship.

Built in honor of the late businessman Mohamed Abdulkhaliq Gargash, the mosque is renowned for its modern and unique design. Designed by prominent architect Sumaya Dabbagh, it stands out as one of the first mosques in the UAE to be designed by a female architect.

The Gargash Mosque is clad in white stone and features special calligraphic elements on its facade. The combination of light, geometry, and modern architecture makes this mosque a highly intriguing building in Dubai. Located in the Al Quoz district, it beautifully blends the interplay of light and form.

Designed by the architect as a place for prayer and spiritual reflection, the Gargash Mosque masterfully integrates light and geometry in a harmonious and inspiring way. It is often referred to as the "Mosque of Light" due to its innovative use of light and shadow. Upon entering the mosque, visitors are welcomed by a shaded courtyard that separates the two main buildings. The larger building houses the magnificent prayer halls, whose domes seem to touch the sky. While the men's prayer room is located on

Mosque of Light

the ground floor, women have their prayer hall on the first floor. In another section of the mosque, there are ablution facilities and living quarters.

Special attention was also given to the sustainability of the project. The entire mosque was built using eco-friendly materials. Locally sourced aluminum and specially imported stone from Oman not only provide the mosque with a solid structure but also contribute to its environmentally conscious design.

Open to the public, the Mosque of Light welcomes visitors of all faiths who wish to perform their prayers or simply enjoy the unique atmosphere of this sacred place.

Good to Know

The mosque is open daily, and admission is free.

How to Get There?

Al Rigga

#40

4h

DUBAI'S SOUKS

Explore a World of Gold, Spices, and Perfumes

Gold Souk

The Gold Souk in Dubai is a traditional market renowned for its impressive selection of gold and jewelry.

Located in the commercial business district of Deira, near the Dubai Creek, the souk stretches through narrow alleys and is a true treasure trove of sparkling gold. With over 380 retailers, primarily dealing in gold and silver, the Gold Souk attracts both locals and tourists seeking exquisite jewelry.

Visitors to the Gold Souk will be captivated by the shimmering displays and intricately designed jewelry. The shops offer a wide variety of gold pieces, including rings, necklaces, bracelets, and earrings, often adorned with precious gemstones. The designs range from traditional to modern,

Star of Taiba at the Gold Souk

Spice Souk

catering to every taste. A true highlight is a visit to the local jeweler Taiba, home to the world's largest gold ring, the "Star of Taiba". This incredible piece is adorned with 5,17 kg of Swarovski crystals and weighs around 60 kg. The "Star of Taiba" holds the Guinness World Record as the largest gold ring in the world.

The Gold Souk is not just a shopping destination but also a significant part of Dubai's cultural identity. It is a bustling marketplace that reflects the region's rich history and trade. In addition to gold jewelry, you can also find silver and platinum items, as well as gemstones and pearls.

Visitors to the Gold Souk should take the time to explore the narrow alleys and discover the treasures of the gold and jewelry world. Prices are usually negotiable, so mastering the art of bargaining is recommended. The vibrant and colorful atmosphere of the Gold Souk makes the shopping experience truly special.

At the Textile Souk, you'll find yourself

Textile Souk

in a paradise of colors and fabrics. Here, you can discover beautifully crafted garments, scarves, and shawls in a seemingly endless variety.

Another highlight is the Spice Souk, where your senses are captivated by the enticing aromas of exotic spices and herbs. Discover a wealth of spices that will enhance your cooking and take your taste buds on a journey. Explore exotic spices such as saffron, cinnamon, turmeric, and cardamom. Let the friendly merchants guide you and learn more about traditional Arabian cuisine. At the Perfume Souk, you'll immerse yourself in the world of fragrances and be enchanted by unique perfumes. From classic to exotic, you'll find everything your heart desires. Wrap yourself in alluring scents and take home a piece of the Orient.

The souks offer not only a unique shopping experience but also insights into the traditional culture and hospitality of Dubai. Stroll through the narrow alleyways where passionate merchants display their goods, and bargaining is a part of daily life. Here,

Perfume Souk

4h Deira

you can not only purchase unique souvenirs but also collect valuable memories.

Before diving into the world of the souks, consider a few important tips: Dress modestly to respect local customs and avoid unwanted attention. Familiarize yourself with the layout of the souks beforehand. Be prepared for vendors competing for your attention, but remain polite and friendly.

Haggling is a tradition here. Negotiate in a friendly manner to get good deals – the initial price is often marked up. Download a currency converter app to easily compare prices to your home currency. It's advisable to carry enough cash, as not all shops accept credit or debit cards. Purchase from vendors with storefronts directly on the market streets to avoid scams and ensure product quality.

Good to Know

The souks are open Sunday to Thursday from 10:00 AM to 10:00 PM, and on Fridays from 4:00 PM to 10:00 PM. Most souks close during the hot midday hours from 1:00 PM to 4:00 PM.

How to Get There?

Al Ras or Al Ghubaiba

#41

4h

VISITING THE GARDEN IN THE SKY AT Dubai Expo City

Curious about what this "Garden in the Sky" is all about?

This unique attraction is located at the Jubilee Pavilion and was one of the most visited spots during Expo 2020. A floating garden that rises up to 55 meters into the air, offering a stunning view over the Expo grounds.

Once lifted into the air, the observation platform slowly rotates, giving you a completely new perspective on Dubai and Expo City. The name "Garden in the Sky" is truly fitting, as the upper level features an enchanting garden like no other. Surrounded by greenery and trees that create a magical atmosphere, it's a perfect spot to capture memorable photos.

Wondering what else you can experience on the former Expo grounds? Even after the Expo, there are still numerous exciting attractions and culinary delights to explore. Stroll through the pavilions and immerse yourself in a world of wonder. Many of the Expo 2020 pavilions are open daily from 12:00 PM to 8:00 PM, offering

Garden in the Sky

Expo 2020 Grounds

plenty of time to explore a world full of marvels. Discover the triumphs of women in history at the Women's Pavilion, or embark on a nostalgic journey through the legacy of Expo 2020 at the "Stories of Nations Pavilion". At the Mobility Pavilion, you can even witness the incredible advancements in artificial intelligence.

And for all the food enthusiasts, there are plenty of culinary delights from around the world. Whether you consider yourself a gourmet or not, Expo City Dubai offers something for every palate. Don't forget to check out Alkebulan, the world's first African dining hall. It features 11 different sections with African restaurants. You can choose from South African barbecue, East African seafood dishes, or Senegalese pastries, all prepared by top African chefs.

Good to Know

The "Garden in the Sky" is open from 6:00 PM to 10:00 PM. The Expo grounds are open 24/7, but most pavilions operate from 12:00 PM to 8:00 PM. Admission for the "Garden in the Sky" costs approximately £7 and is free for children under 2 years old. The Expo City day pass costs around £30 per person and provides access to all pavilions on the grounds. Children under 12 can enter for free. Access to the Surreal Water Pavilion and Al Wasl Plaza is free for everyone (for more information, visit expocitydubai.com).

How to Get There?

Expo 2020

#42

8h

Lego fun for the whole family at **LEGOLAND DUBAI**

In Legoland Dubai, families can enjoy a magical experience filled with Lego bricks and thrilling water slides.

This theme park, designed especially for children aged 2 to 12, is divided into two main areas – the Lego Park and the Lego Water Park. With nearly 40 interactive rides, 20 water slides, and over 15,000 Lego models to explore, there's plenty to keep everyone entertained. Visit the

Factory to learn how Lego bricks are made, build your own models, and take home a freshly made Lego set as a souvenir.

In Lego City, you can drive Lego cars, fly planes, and sail boats while kids earn their very own Legoland driver's license. The Kingdoms transport you to a world of dragons, castles, and medieval adventure. Enjoy a thrilling rollercoaster ride or hop on pirate-themed carousels. In the "Imagination" zone, build Lego cars and race them, or dive into mechanics and robotics. Watch a 4D movie at the theater and join fun training and programming workshops. The Adventure area lets you explore the underwater world in a submarine, see over 1,500 marine creatures, and embark on exciting treasure hunts inspired by Egyptian mythology. Don't miss Mini-Land, where you can marvel at a Lego-built version of Dubai's skyline.

Enjoy a playful day in the vibrant world of LEGO adventures and create magical memories with your family full of fun and joy.

Good to Know

Legoland Park is open from 10:00 AM to 6:00 PM, while the Lego Water Park stays open until 7:00 PM. A day pass for either the Lego Park or the Lego Water Park costs about £65 each. However, we recommend the combo ticket (Lego Park + Lego Water Park), which is approximately £75 total. Be aware that tickets purchased at the gate are more expensive than those bought online. Children under 3 years old enter for free, and there are occasional promotions where kids accompanying adults also enter free of charge. It's worth checking the website for current offers (www.legoland.com/dubai).

How to Get There?

You can take bus line DPR1 to The Outlet Village stop, from where it's about a 10-minute walk to the park. Alternatively, we recommend taking a taxi or driving, as ample parking is available.

#93

2h

Breathtaking Desert Sunrise

EXPERIENCE A HOT AIR BALLOON RIDE

Experience an unforgettable adventure in the sky with a hot air balloon ride – one of Dubai's most spectacular activities.

Float peacefully above the desert as the unique landscape of Dubai unfolds before your eyes. The balloon rides offer a variety of flight packages to suit every preference. Opt for the deluxe sunrise flights to witness the sun rising over the Hajar Mountains as you glide through the sky. Private flights are perfect for romantic getaways or unique marriage proposals. Experienced pilots ensure a safe and enjoyable journey, pointing out landmarks and sharing their knowledge about the region. A special highlight is the exclusive in-flight falcon show, included in all packages.

Great emphasis is placed on top-quality hot air balloons, which are regularly maintained to meet the highest safety standards. Equipped with state-of-the-art technology, the balloons ensure a smooth and comfortable ride.

The flights often start early in the morning to catch the spectacular sunrise over the desert landscapes. During the ride, you'll have the chance to admire the surroundings from a bird's-eye view and may even spot animals like camels wandering below. Some tours also combine additional experiences, such as a ride in a vintage Land Rover and a delicious breakfast after landing.

Good to Know

Hot air balloon rides take place in the early morning hours to enjoy the spectacular sunrise experience. A hot air balloon trip costs around £230 per person. We recommend the provider "Hot Air Balloon Dubai", which has already won a TripAdvisor Travellers' Choice Award (more information on www.hotairballoonuae.com).

How to Get There?

Depending on the package, you can benefit from a premium pick-up and drop-off service for your trip.

#44

2h

EXPERIENCE THRILLING CAMEL

Races with Robot Jockeys

Experience the thrill and excitement of camel racing in Dubai, a truly unique local tradition that you can enjoy during your holiday in the city.

Believe it or not, this traditional sporting event not only captures the curiosity of visitors but also brings together locals from all Emirates of the UAE.

Imagine watching trained racing camels, with robot-controlled jockeys, speeding along desert tracks at about 65 km/h. These camel races have a centuries-old tradition, where people from Middle Eastern communities would gather during festivals and events like weddings to participate in this popular sport. Much like horse racing, the camels compete against each other as they race along a designated track.

And now, the high-tech aspect comes into play. Since 2002, human jockeys have been banned from camel racing in the UAE, replaced by lightweight, robot-controlled jockeys. Believe it or not, these robots, decorated in team colors, are mounted on the camels and equipped with a wireless cordless screwdriver attached to a whip that encourages the camel to run faster without causing harm. Dubai's camel racing season typically takes place during the cooler winter months, from October to April, across various tracks throughout the country. The races are usually held in the early morning hours or sometimes in the afternoon.

Camel races are generally free to attend. Arrive early on race day and take advantage of the opportunity to snap photos with the camels. Dubai's largest racecourse is the Al Marmoom Camel Race Track, located near the Al Marmoum Heritage Village.

Good to Know

Camel races are typically free to attend. The races usually take place early in the morning at 7:00 AM or in the afternoon at 2:00 PM (for more information on current races, visit www.dubaicrc.ae). The races typically last around 15 minutes, followed by the awards ceremony.

How to Get There?

Some buses, like bus route 66, go out to the Al Marmoon Camel Race Track. Get off at the Al Fathan Masjid 1 stop.

#45

4h

A Journey Around the World at GLOBAL VILLAGE

Discover an unparalleled journey around the globe in one place - Global Village Dubai warmly invites you to explore the many facets of different cultures, spanning from Europe and Asia to the Americas.

An extraordinary shopping and entertainment paradise awaits you and your entire family. Here, you can explore more than 75 countries in over 30 pavilions, immersing yourself in the wonders of history and diverse cultures. Marvel at the iconic backdrops of ancient Egypt, admire the majestic grandeur of London's Palace of Westminster, and be enchanted by the unmistakable beauty of Italy's Leaning Tower of Pisa. Global Village blends colors, flavors, and experiences from all corners of the world. Open from October to April, this

Russia in the Global Village

theme park offers a wealth of cultural experiences, entertainment, dining, and shopping options, making it a place where visitors can travel the world without leaving Dubai.

During the winter season, Global Village opens its gates and warmly welcomes visitors to an impressive fairground with over 100 thrilling rides. The theme park creates a lively carnival atmosphere with dazzling lights and sensational attractions for your enjoyment. A standout highlight is the "Wheel of the World" Ferris wheel, adorned with LED lights, where you can enjoy a relaxing ride in one of its 30 gondolas.

But Global Village offers much more than just fun and excitement. For shopaholics, it's a true paradise. In the numerous pavilions, you can discover souvenirs, delicacies, and handicrafts from around the globe. From exquisite wood carvings from Africa to aromatic spices from India and handcrafted carpets from Iran, there's something for everyone. Sample the unique flavor of Yemeni Sidr honey, one of the most expensive honeys in the world, or savor delicious dried fruits from Thailand. For beauty lovers, there are popular products like Moroccan argan oil to indulge in.

Food lovers will also find their paradise at Global Village. With over 23 restaurants and cafés, it offers a wide range of international dishes. From authentic Indian tandoori chicken to hearty Bosnian ćevapčići and the tantalizing aromas of street food stalls, there's a world of flavors waiting to be explored. Don't forget to try the traditional Emirati coffee and visit the unique floating market, where tuk-tuks and abras serve a variety of delicious treats.

But Global Village wouldn't be complete without its remarkable events. Each season, exciting performances are expected, including spectacular stunt shows, cultural performances, and captivating street art. Highlights include the Superloop stunt show and grand circus performances. Additionally, enjoy free concerts on the open-air main stage featuring international stars.

Good to Know

Global Village is typically open from October to April, daily from 4:00 PM to midnight (and even one hour longer on weekends). Admission is approximately £4 per person, with free entry for children under 3 and seniors over 65 (more details available at www.globalvillage.ae).

How to Get There?

Located on Sheikh Mohammed bin Zayed Road in the southeast of the city, we recommend traveling by taxi or your own rental car.

#96

4h

Discover the
Blooming Beauty of the
DUBAI MIRACLE GARDEN

Step into the incredible world of the Dubai Miracle Garden, an idyllic flower garden in the middle of the desert, which has captured the hearts of visitors from around the world since its opening in 2013.

This enchanting park impresses with its unique display of real flowers that thrive even in the scorching heat. Explore an oasis of colors and shapes adorned with massive floral sculptures - from a majestic flower castle to an astonishing flower airplane and a unique floral clock.

The Dubai Miracle Garden is a place that constantly evolves, offering new surprises with each visit. Every year, new sculptures and fascinating themes are created to spark the imagination of visitors. This makes the garden a spot you'll want to revisit, as there's always something new to discover. To make the most of your visit, it's recommended to arrive

An Emirates A-380
Plane Made of Flowers

The Smurfs at Miracle Garden

early, especially in the morning when the crowds are smaller. For a truly special experience, you can also explore the Dubai Miracle Garden in the evening under the enchanting glow of the garden's lights.

Dubai Miracle Garden is not just a place of flowers but also a hub of world records. Among its most impressive features is the enormous replica of an Emirates Airbus A-380, covered in a staggering 5 million flowers, making it a world-record-breaking floral display. You'll also find other awe-inspiring elements, from beloved Disney characters like Donald Duck and Mickey Mouse to a floral recreation of the iconic Burj Khalifa, all adding to the garden's unique charm.

For families with children, Dubai Miracle Garden is a magical wonderland. The Disney character sculptures bring smiles to young visitors, while hammocks offer cozy spots for relaxing breaks. The auditorium stage hosts enchanting performances, and the trampoline area guarantees pure fun for kids. The well-maintained, flat pathways also make it easy to navigate with strollers throughout the park.

Dubai Miracle Garden is wheelchair accessible, with the exception of the castle in the center of the park. Special care has been taken to ensure that the paths are smooth and easy to navigate, allowing all visitors to fully experience the stunning floral displays.

In addition to the breathtaking blooms of Dubai Miracle Garden, visitors can also explore the nearby Butterfly Garden. This enchanting paradise features 9 domes, each home to vibrant butterflies of various species. The climate-controlled domes of the Dubai Butterfly Garden house over 15,000 butterflies from more than 45 species. With a pleasant year-round temperature of 18-25°C, it's an ideal environment for visitors, plants, and butterflies alike. The "Dubai Butterfly Garden Kids Cinema" offers a selection of educational films and animations about butterflies, perfect for young visitors.

Be sure to visit the amazing gallery of handcrafted artworks made from thousands of butterflies. These pieces range from replicas of classic art to large portraits. When a butterfly passes away, the team takes great care to preserve its natural state. It is then incorporated into a larger artwork that blends human creativity with the beauty of nature, creating stunning masterpieces that honor both art and the natural world.

Good to Know

Tickets for the Dubai Miracle Garden are approximately £17 for adults and £13 for children under 12. Children under 3 can enter for free (more information at www.dubaimiraclegarden.com). Tickets for the Butterfly Garden are around £13 per person (more details at www.dubaibutterflygarden.com). Both gardens are open during the winter months, typically from October/November to April or May. During this period, they are open daily from 9:00 AM to 6:00 PM, though times may vary by season, so it's best to check the respective websites beforehand.

How to Get There?

Mall of the Emirates

From the Mall of the Emirates Metro Station, you can take bus F36 to the Arjan, Sheraton Building 1 stop.

#47

4h

A Hidden Gem

CAMEL RIDING WITH CAMEL USCHI

Ursula Musch, known as "Camel Uschi", is widely recognized in Dubai for her work on her camel farm and her efforts to share the rich heritage of Arabian culture and traditions.

Her camel farm hosts exclusive events, photoshoots, and traditional desert evenings, with camel riding being one of the main attractions. The farm has become a popular destination for tourists seeking an authentic experience with camels and the desert culture, providing a genuine insight into the region's traditions.

Ursula Musch has gained a certain level of recognition through her long-standing work and presence in Dubai. She has been featured in media reports and even on German TV shows like "Goodbye Germany!" Her dedication to running her camel farm and promoting local culture earned her the nickname "Camel Uschi".

With over 30 camels on her farm, she is widely known for her expertise in camel breeding and is regarded as a prominent figure in preserving the customs and traditions of the Emirates. Visitors are invited to experience genuine Bedouin hospitality and immerse themselves in the rich culture of this remarkable region. Upon arrival, you'll be warmly welcomed with a traditional serving of Arabic tea and date cookies, following long-standing desert customs. You'll also have the chance to explore the farm at your

own pace and, depending on the timing of your visit, witness the camel feeding.

Many of the camels on the farm are accustomed to human interaction and can be gently touched upon request. As you explore the farm, you'll also have the opportunity to taste delicious camel milk.

Before the camel ride begins, you will receive a brief introduction covering the course of the excursion, safety rules, and a quick overview of camel riding techniques. Once you're ready, the adventure begins. You'll be seated on one of Camel Uschi's camels, and an experienced camel handler will guide and accompany your ride. The desert landscape of Dubai provides a breathtaking backdrop for your adventure. During the tour, you'll have the chance to admire the beauty of the desert, and your guide may share fascinating stories about camel breeding and the cultural significance of camels in the region. Your camel guide will ensure that you are comfortable and will be happy to answer any questions you may have. There are often stops along the way to take stunning photos of you on the camel, set against the picturesque desert scenery.

After the camel tour concludes, you will be brought back to Camel Uschi's base. You can choose to relax either in a cozy Bedouin tent or on the picturesque surrounding dunes, allowing yourself to be mesmerized by the enchanting beauty of the desert–especially during the glowing sunsets in the evening. If you wish to indulge in the flavors of the region, there is also an option to enjoy delicious Arabic dishes, such as freshly baked flatbread, Fasolia (beans), or grilled meats.

Good to Know

A 1-hour camel ride, including a 1-hour farm visit, costs about £62. You also have the option to add an Emirati meal, bringing the total to approximately £100. The "Desert Magic" experience (an evening in the desert, lasting around 5 hours) costs about £140 (more information at en.kameluschi.com). Regular camel rides are available daily, while the camel ride with Emirati meal is only bookable on Thursdays and Fridays. The "Desert Magic" experience is only available on Saturdays.

How to Get There?

The farm is located about 30 to 60 minutes from Dubai, and we recommend traveling by taxi or rental car.

#48

4h

SKYDIVING
Above the Desert

Dubai offers not only breathtaking views on land and sea but also an unparalleled experience in the sky.

What could be more thrilling than the opportunity to leap out of an airplane from a height of 4,000 meters, hurtling through the air at an astonishing speed of around 200 km/h in free fall? Fulfill your dream of skydiving and experience this intense adventure during your next visit to Dubai.

For beginners, the experience includes a tandem skydive, where you are securely strapped to an experienced instructor throughout the entire jump. However, if you hold a skydiving license, you'll have the option to jump solo. Before the jump, you'll register, receive the necessary safety equipment,

and go through a detailed briefing to ensure your comfort and safety.

You'll then ascend to about 4,000 meter, marking the start of your exhilarating adventure. Accompanied by a professional instructor and supported by an additional expert who will capture the entire experience on video, you'll embark on the jump of a lifetime. During the first 60 seconds, you'll experience the incredible rush of free fall. Once you reach about 1,800 meter, your parachute will be deployed, allowing for a safe descent. You can then enjoy a breathtaking bird's-eye view for approximately 4 to 5 minutes before safely landing. You'll receive your edited jump video via email within 48 hours, and for a small additional fee, the video can be optimized and edited for Instagram.

SkyDive Dubai is regarded as the leading provider of outdoor skydiving experiences in Dubai. The team consists of highly qualified instructors and experienced skydivers. SkyDive Dubai offers two fantastic locations for your skydiving adventure. The "Palm Zone" provides a spectacular view of Dubai's skyline, including iconic landmarks such as the Palm Jumeirah, Burj Al Arab, and the Atlantis Hotel. Alternatively, you can opt for the "Desert Zone" experience, where you'll be dropped over the vast Dubai desert along the Al Ain Road. From here, you'll have the opportunity to admire the endless sand dunes and catch a glimpse of Dubai's glittering skyline in the distance.

Good to Know

The tandem skydiving experience isn't exactly cheap, but it's definitely an adventure that will stay with you for a lifetime. The cost of a tandem skydive ranges from about £400 to £500, depending on the zone you choose. Please note that the jump is only allowed for those aged 12 and above, and you must be in good health and physically fit to participate. Booking is available online, and reservations must be made in advance (more info on www.skydivedubai.ae).

How to Get There?

Sobha Realty

The skydive locations are the Palm Zone (Sobha Realty Metro Station) and the Desert Zone (recommended to arrive by taxi or rental car).

#49

4h

Flamingo Watching

AT RAS AL KHOR WILDLIFE SANCTUARY

The Ras Al Khor Wildlife Sanctuary, also known as the "Cape of the Creek", is a fenced nature reserve famous for attracting a large number of birds.

Spanning a vast area, it is home to a diverse range of wildlife, including crustaceans, small mammals, and fish. The sanctuary provides a protected urban environment in the heart of Dubai and serves as an important habitat for many species, especially migratory birds that rest here during their journeys. During the winter months, the sanctuary becomes a magical place with flocks of pink flamingos, which are particularly abundant. The sanctuary also contains a variety of ecosystems, including mangroves, lagoons, reed beds, and shrublands.

Ras Al Khor Wildlife Sanctuary offers visitors the chance to observe birds and other animals in their natural habitat. There are three bird-watching hides located at prime spots, giving visitors a close-up view of the wildlife. One of them is the "Mangrove Hide", where you can get an up-close look at the tropical mangroves and, during the winter months, spot ducks, spoonbills, cormorants, greenshanks, and, if you're lucky, even storks.

As the name suggests, the "Flamingo Hide" allows you to admire the graceful pink flamingos up close. Lastly, the "Lagoon Hide" is a truly serene spot where you can enjoy a unique panoramic view of the shimmering waters of the Creek, while discovering a rich variety of birds of prey, waterbirds, and much more.

Good to Know

The sanctuary is open daily from 7:30 AM to 5:30 PM and can be visited free of charge.

How to Get There?

Ras Al Khor Wildlife Sanctuary is located at 58RF+G32 - Ras Al Khor Rd. We recommend getting there by taxi or rental car.

#50

4h

Desert Romance at LOVE LAKE DUBAI

Discover the unique Love Lake Dubai - perhaps the most romantic spot in the city.

Located in the heart of the Al Qudra desert, Love Lake Dubai has been enchanting visitors since its opening in 2018 with its two interconnected heart-shaped lakes. Due to its vast size, the full beauty of the lakes can only be appreciated from above. The entire area is dedicated to the theme of love, adorned with heart-shaped signs and motifs throughout.

Love Lake is much more than just a spot for barbecues or evening strolls. It's undoubtedly one of Dubai's most innovative attractions. The tranquility, peaceful, and romantic setting, far from the bustling city, make it a popular choice for couples of all ages.

Here, you'll find absolute peace and relaxation. Nestled in the dunes, it offers one of the most breathtaking sunsets in Dubai. The warm orange hues of the sun, the golden sand, and the greenery are hard to put into words, making the best time to visit about an hour before sunset. Over 16,000 trees and plants surround Love Lake, with even the branches of the trees and shrubs shaped into hearts.

The park is perfect for walking and picnicking. You can dip your feet in the water and use signs to identify the shallow areas of the lake. Part of the lake is a fishpond where koi fish and goldfish reside. Though the koi fish may appear intimidating with their large mouths, they don't bite. Please note that fishing is strictly prohibited and subject to fines. There are also numerous photogenic spots throughout Love Lake Park, all heart-shaped, making it a beautiful setting for memorable photos.

Visit Love Lake to immerse yourself in the tranquility, nature, calm waters, and the variety of birds living here. Far from the bustling city life of Dubai, Love Lake is a place of relaxation, good for your lungs and heart. It also serves as a habitat for desert animals like foxes and gazelles. Here, you can rediscover romance, strengthen

family bonds, and share hearty laughter. Time seems to almost stand still in this serene environment.

The relaxation and peace that Love Lake Dubai offers make it an ideal spot for barbecues as well. Although there are no fixed grilling stations, you're welcome to bring your own. As night falls, the air fills with the rich aromas of slow-cooked meats and vegetables as grills are lit. The Middle Eastern barbecue culture is well-known for fostering family connections, respect for elders, and social gatherings–all of which are beautifully reflected at Love Lake.

Camping overnight at Love Lake is especially rewarding and completely free. Take advantage of this unique opportunity to camp at Love Lake if you want to wake up to the sun, birds, and wildlife. Sleep under the open sky in a tent and enjoy the gentle breeze. Don't worry, there are no creepy-crawlies around. Early morning bird calls will gently wake you, giving you the chance to witness a stunning sunrise with a cup of coffee in hand. Even as you say goodbye to Love Lake, you'll be greeted by hundreds of swans, ducks, and other waterfowl.

For a comfortable overnight stay, you'll need a tent, light bulbs or a lantern, a flashlight, pillows, blankets, and drinking water. A light pajama set is perfect for summer, while you should bring warm clothing if you're camping in the winter.

Love Lake Dubai stands as a testament to Dubai's eco-friendly vision.

Every part of the lake is designed with sustainability in mind. The park benches and tissue boxes are made from biodegradable materials, and you can even spot sinks crafted from bamboo and wood.

The amenities at Love Lake Dubai include a designated area called Hadirah, which offers picnic spots, running water, barbecue areas, restrooms, and benches. The park also features three jogging tracks that span over 7 km, illuminated after dark, making it ideal for evening runs. Even the stones marking the path are heart-shaped. A detailed map of the lake and park is engraved on a wooden board near the entrance.

There are currently no shops or restaurants near Love Lake, so be sure to bring food and water with you when visiting. While there are no streetlights, you'll find plenty of wooden park benches to relax and take in the view. For a bit of fun, there are swings made from large tree branches, though these are not suitable for small children.

Love Lake wouldn't be complete without the nearby "Last Exit", a unique open-air food truck park concept located about a 15-minute drive from the lake. Here, you can enjoy exotic dishes from various cuisines served directly to your vehicle from food trucks, so there's no need to get out of the car. Additionally, there are small play areas for kids. During winter, many children play in this charming park while adults savor delicious meals at makeshift tables and chairs. The atmosphere is laid-back and relaxed. There's also a gas station nearby, as well as a large camping supply store for all your outdoor needs. The "Last Exit" is a perfect stop before heading back from the wilderness of Love Lake.

Good to Know

The park is free to access and open 24 hours a day.

How to Get There?

Love Lake is located about a 40-minute drive from Dubai and is best reached with a 4x4 vehicle. There is ample parking available on-site. Alternatively, the tour operator Viator offers a guided tour with pick-up and drop-off for around £110 per person (simply search "Love Lake Dubai" on www.viator.com).

#51

4h

Explore the World's Deepest Dive Pool at DEEP DIVE DUBAI

Deep Dive Dubai is the deepest diving pool in the world, officially recognized by the Guinness Book of Records.

Visit an astonishing underwater world and embark on an unparalleled adventure, open to both beginners and certified divers alike. The diving center offers thrilling opportunities to explore a sunken city, inspired by the rich pearl-diving tradition of the United Arab Emirates. To celebrate this heritage, the building is designed in the shape of an oyster, paying tribute to the nation's past as a hub for pearl diving.

Dive to a record-breaking depth of 60 meters and explore an underwater world full of wonders. The massive indoor pool is filled with 14 million liter of fresh water, the equivalent of six Olympic swimming pools. With a constant water temperature of 30°C, ideal diving conditions are maintained, eliminating the need for thick wetsuits.

The sunken city is a unique attraction, adding an enchanting element to the diving experience. Be captivated by the mystical theme as you navigate through the labyrinth of underwater streets and buildings. Modern lighting and sound effects create a magical atmosphere that will leave you in awe. Experienced diving experts are always by your side, offering valuable tips to help you make the most of your dive.

The water is filtered every six hours to maintain the highest hygiene standards. The dive center features the largest and most advanced hyperbaric chamber in the region, ensuring quick assistance in the highly unlikely event of a diving accident. With numerous underwater cameras monitoring divers throughout their experience, safety is guaranteed as you explore the unique underwater world.

Visitors can watch the divers in the massive pool through large windows or on screens inside the building. After your dive, relax in the cozy café on the "B2" floor, where you can enjoy a view of the sunken city through the large glass panels that overlook the dive pool.

Good to Know

Deep Dive Dubai is open daily from 9:00 AM to 6:00 PM. Prices range from approximately £250 to £655, depending on the dive you choose. If you prefer not to dive, snorkeling is available for around £85. All necessary dive equipment is provided, so you only need to bring your swimwear (more details can be found at www.deepdivedubai.com). Please note that after a dive, it is advised not to skydive or fly the next day.

How to Get There?

Deep Dive Dubai is located in Nad Al Sheba 1. Since it's not well-connected by public transportation, taking a taxi or driving a rental car is recommended.

#52

4h

Visit the Award-Winning The Farm **RESTAURANT IN AL BARARI**

Discover the enchanting world of Al Barari and visit the unique The Farm Restaurant. Step into a green paradise in the heart of Dubai, and immerse yourself in an oasis of tranquility and nature.

Al Barari, meaning "wilderness" in Arabic, was born from a vision to create a botanical oasis in a city better known for its desert landscape. Over time, seven extraordinary gardens were developed, transforming this part of Dubai into a true floral haven.

At the heart of this green oasis lies The Farm Restaurant. Featuring a mix of indoor and outdoor seating, floor-to-ceiling windows, and views of the water garden, it offers a space of relaxation and indulgence. The beautifully designed restaurant leaves no visitor unmoved, and its diverse menu – from continental to healthy and authentic Thai cuisine – will captivate you. The Farm has earned a stellar reputation, winning numerous awards for its outstanding performance, including "Restaurant of the Year - Healthy Food", "Most Romantic Restaurant", and "Best Modern European Restaurant under 100€", among others. The farm-to-table concept emphasizes high-quality, natural ingredients transformed into delicious dishes that are both sustainable and healthy. In a serene and peaceful setting, you can enjoy a culinary experience like no other. The Farm also offers exciting activities such as art and cooking classes, or how about an afternoon tea in good company? Even exclusive jewelry presentations take place here, surrounded by the unique flora and fauna that inspire The Farm.

Enjoy wellness and relaxation at the adjacent Body Language Health Club, which features a state-of-the-art fitness center, tennis courts, and an infinity pool. From yoga classes to various fitness offerings, this club has everything to help align body and mind. The villas in Al Barari, surrounded by lush greenery, offer a perfect blend of Islamic and modern architecture. The complex includes various residential areas, with diverse plant life lovingly maintained by skilled gardeners. The development is set to expand with plans for hotels, schools, and medical facilities. Al Barari is not just a residential area or a restaurant; it's a unique social hub for nature lovers, health enthusiasts, and wellness seekers.

Good to Know

The Farm Restaurant is open daily from 7:30 AM to 10:30 PM. Breakfast is served from 7:30 AM to 11:30 AM, lunch from 12:00 PM to 3:30 PM, and the evening menu is available from 6:00 PM to 10:30 PM. Ordering is conveniently done via a modern iPad in the restaurant, and the friendly and helpful staff add to the experience. If you want to get a taste of what's in store, check out the delicious food photos at www.thefarmdubai.ae.

How to Get There?

We recommend getting there by taxi or rental car. The restaurant is located on Warsan 3 Road.

#53

8h

Experience Superheroes, Dinosaurs, and Thrills at **IMG WORLDS OF ADVENTURE**

Experience an extraordinary day full of joy and adventure at IMG Worlds of Adventure, the largest indoor theme park in the world.

The park is a truly spectacular experience for all ages. Every day, it welcomes more than 20,000 visitors and offers four unique themed zones, known as "Epic Zones".

In the first zone, embark on a magical journey back to your childhood and meet beloved cartoon characters that you grew up with. This area is a true paradise for cartoon fans, offering thrilling rides and unforgettable character encounters.

The second zone is a haven for Marvel fans. Immerse yourself in the thrilling world of superheroes and experience fantastic rides straight from the movies. Feel the excitement as you spin on the "Thor Thunder Spin" or engage in a heart-pounding chase like in a real Avengers adventure. This zone is a tribute to the most popular heroes of the Marvel universe and is sure to captivate you.

If you have a fascination for the prehistoric world, the third zone, known as "The Lost Valley", is perfect for you. Step into a world filled with dinosaurs and feel like an explorer of ancient times. Thrilling rides like the Velociraptor and Adventure Fortress will get your heart racing and satisfy your thirst for adventure.

And last but not least, the fourth zone offers a spine-chilling experience like no other. Enter the park's infamous Haunted Hotel – if you dare – and face your fears on exciting horror rides. This area is ideal for those seeking an adrenaline rush and an unforgettable time in a spooky, dark atmosphere.

In addition to the rides, the park also offers a wide variety of themed restaurants where you can enjoy delicious meals. From cartoon-inspired dishes to superhero-themed menus, there's something to satisfy every taste.

Good to Know

The park is open Sunday to Thursday from 12:00 PM to 10:00 PM, and on Fridays and Saturdays, it's open until 11:00 PM. Tickets cost approximately £75 per person.

How to Get There?

IMG Worlds of Adventure is located on the E311 (Sheikh Mohammed Bin Zayed Road - near Arabian Ranches, next to Global Village). We recommend traveling by taxi or rental car.

#54

8h+

Luxurious Desert Camping at **NEST BY SONARA**

The origins of Nara Desert Escape stem from founder Stephanie Reichenbach's passion for the desert.

Her vision was to create an authentic, elegant, and eco-friendly desert camping experience for everyone. This vision was brought to life with the unique overnight concept known as "Nest by Sonara", where guests are invited to immerse themselves in the serene and mindful experience of "Desert Nesting".

This unique experience allows visitors to fully immerse themselves in the beauty of the desert while staying in exclusive accommodations nestled within the desert dunes. The "Nest" is a private and tranquil oasis, offering

guests the chance to enjoy the starlit sky and the serenity of the desert during an overnight stay.

Nara Desert Escape is proud to be located within the stunning Dubai Desert Conservation Reserve (DDCR), a sanctuary of breathtaking landscapes, native flora and fauna, and a haven for antelope and gazelles.

The "Nest by Sonara" offers an exclusive atmosphere, ideal for travelers seeking peace and relaxation in the heart of the desert. This luxury glamping option allows guests to stay in a unique setting while enjoying the comforts of a premium experience. Each Nest is equipped with a private bathroom and a terrace, and the main bed is a cozy double. An additional

bed can be arranged, accommodating up to 2 adults and 2 children, ensuring comfort for families and couples alike.

The in-house chef has crafted a signature menu, served in the evening at the main bar. Breakfast is offered at dawn, and guests also have the option to dine at the Sonara Camp, enjoying an evening filled with entertainment. Perched atop a dune, the open-air bar offers breathtaking views of the desert, allowing you to witness a stunning sunset. Guests can enjoy a variety of beverages, including cocktails, wines, and appetizers, in a relaxed desert setting.

For a unique experience, don't miss the "Sky Safari" at the camp. This fascinating activity enhances your knowledge of astronomy while connecting you to the history and heritage of the Arab world. Learn why astronomy is so significant in the Middle East and observe galaxies, stars, distant nebulas, and planets. Test your newfound knowledge while sitting around a cozy campfire with hot chocolate and roasted marshmallows.

Good to Know

The "Nests" are typically open from September to June. While the luxurious Nara "desert nests" are not the most affordable, we believe it offers a truly once-in-a-lifetime experience. Prices start at around £385 per nest per night (up to 4 people are allowed per nest). Keep in mind that the 14 nests are designed to provide a peaceful retreat. For more details, visit www.nara.ae.

How to Get There?

The entrance to the camp is located at the DDCR Gate. We recommend adding a shuttle service to your reservation, which will pick you up in Dubai and bring you back after your stay.

#55

8h

Discover Dubai's Cultural Heritage at

HATTA HERITAGE VILLAGE

The Hatta Heritage Village is a reconstruction of a traditional mountain village located in Hatta, nestled in the Al Hajar Mountains, about 130 km from Dubai.

The village offers a glimpse into the lifestyle and culture of the region's early inhabitants. It has been carefully restored and preserved to maintain its historical ambiance, allowing visitors to explore the heritage of the UAE.

Hatta Heritage Village comprises around 30 traditional buildings, including houses, watchtowers, and a fort. The village showcases various aspects of traditional life in the mountains, including agricultural practices, craftsmanship, and architectural designs.

One of the main highlights is the Bait Al Wali, one of the largest buildings in the village that was once home to a local ruler. It provides insights into the historical governance and administration of the region. Visitors can also explore the original Hatta Fort, dating back to 1896, which is part of the village reconstruction. Additionally, the village features a museum displaying a collection of traditional Emirati tools, clothing, weapons, musical instruments, crafts, and artwork.

Hatta Heritage Village has become a popular tourist attraction, offering visitors a chance to better understand the history and culture of the UAE. It also provides an opportunity to experience traditional crafts such as

Hatta Heritage Village

The Fort at
Hatta Heritage Village

weaving, pottery, and blacksmithing. The surrounding Al Hajar Mountains add to the scenic beauty, creating a picturesque backdrop for cultural and historical exploration.

If you have more time, a visit to the nearby Al-Sharia site is also recommended. This is a palm farm with a special underground irrigation system designed to promote crop and tree growth, even in times of limited rainfall, ensuring the livelihood and well-being of the local community.

Before organizing your visit, please note that there are no cafés or restaurants within Hatta Heritage Village. Therefore, it is advisable to bring your own food and beverages. It's highly recommended to plan your trip during the cooler months, particularly from September to March, to avoid the extremely high temperatures. Additionally, arriving early in the morning is better to avoid the intense sun in the mountainous regions.

A visit to Hatta Heritage Village offers a remarkable exploration of Emirati history and a rewarding experience for culture enthusiasts. Even for those seeking a break from the modernity of Dubai, this cultural contrast, filled with traditions and heritage, proves to be highly recommended.

Good to Know

Hatta Heritage Village is open from Saturday to Thursday, 7:30 AM to 8:30 PM, and on Fridays from 2:30 PM to 8:30 PM. Entry is free of charge.

How to Get There?

Located about 130 km from Dubai in the Hajar Mountains, Hatta Heritage Village is a bit of a distance from the city. We recommend joining an organized tour for the best experience. If you're driving on your own, the journey takes approximately 2 hours. Viator offers several popular tours to Hatta Heritage Village, with prices starting around £85 per person. For more information, visit www.viator.com and search for "Hatta Heritage Village".

IMPRINT

Gamikaze Scheidegger
Pascal Scheidegger
Adlerstrasse 1
8600 Dubendorf
Switzerland
Commercial register / Zurich: CHE-467.312.860 MWST

Cover design and typesetting: Gamikaze Scheidegger

Cover motifs: Alamy/©Kairi Aun, Adobe Stock/©Kertu, Adobe Stock/©Alexey Stio, Adobe Stock/©Oleg Zhukov, Adobe Stock/©saiko3p, Depositphotos/©OlgaTrushkina1, Depositphotos/©bloodua

Paperback ISBN: 978-3-907463-11-6

info@gamikaze.ch
www.gamikaze.ch

GAMIKAZE

PHOTO CREDITS

Photos from Depositphotos:
P. 5 Litteralis, p. 7 Tiko0305, p. 8 Iakov, p. 12 sarathmaroliknr@gmail.com, p. 15 bloodua, p. 22 Paha_L, p. 23 tupungato, p. 25 NewAfrica, p. 34+35 clicksbyabrar, p. 38 bloodua, p. 40+41 Roxana, p. 49 sarathmaroliknr@gmail.com, p. 60+61 bloodua, p. 66 mathes, p. 72 pio3, p. 86+87 deep76, p. 114 frantic00, p. 116+117 CreativeFamily, p. 130 adriaticphoto, p. 132+133 weissdergeier, p. 134 alan64, p. 138 AndrewDonskikh, p. 139 slava296, p. 140 Leonid_Andronov, p. 145 Variant, p. 148 frantic00, p. 152 efesenko, p. 156 Kinderkz, p. 160 apid, p. 168 OlgaTrushkina1, p. 169 alan64, p. 178 d.travnikov, p. 182 alexeys, p. 192 maria.uspen, p. 195 fokkebok, p. 204+205+206+219 CreativeFamily

Adobe Stock:
P. 6 Anita Gläßner, p. 11 Rastislav Sedlak SK, p. 14 Oleg Zhukov, p. 18 KajzrPhotography.com, p. 19 somegirl, p. 20 Food Shop, p. 21 ernestos, p. 24 DenPhoto, p. 27 Alexey Stiop, p. 32+33 creativefamily, p. 37 aleksc, p. 47 pierrick, p. 50+51 Andrey Popov, p. 52+53 Captured Blinks, p. 54 Kertu, p. 64 aleksandar kamasi, p. 65 francis92, p. 70 Jainfo, p. 74+75 diy13, p. 76 kubikactive, p. 78+79 Photocreo Bednarek, p. 80 saiko3p, p. 88+89+90 Frederique, p. 91 manowar1973, p. 92+93 Grigory Bruev, p. 96 Iurii Seleznev, p. 100+101+102 saiko3p, p. 110 dannyburn, p. 112 creativefamily, p. 118 esherez, p. 120+121 neiezhmakov, p. 122 Cagkan, p. 125 Patryk Kosmider, p. 128+129 Simon, p. 136 esherez, p. 150+151 Roman Sigaev, p. 155 diy13, p. 158 ViDi Studio, p. 161 Four_Lakes, p. 171 Tetiana, p. 172+173 farawayroute, p. 184+185 Kisika, p. 186 Bernadett, p. 190 F8 \ Suport Ukraine, p. 196 Steve Lovegrove, p. 198+199 Viktor, p. 212 meen_na, p. 220 lic0001

GNU Free Documentation License
(https://en.wikipedia.org/wiki/GNU_Free_Documentation_License)::
P. 42 Diego Delso

Creative Commons (https://en.wikipedia.org/wiki/Creative_Commons):
P. 16 Shahroozporia, p. 17 Dekoelie, p. 42 Håkan Dahlström, p. 43 Misteruae, p. 46 heyexplorer.com, p. 58 Saaremees, p. 82+83 Filipe Fortes, p. 84 Frank Seiplax, p. 85 Davide Mauro, p. 86 Ank Kumar, p. 94+95 Saaremee, p. 98 Saaremees, p. 104+105+106 WikiSilky, p. 124 7777777kz, p. 140 Studio Sarah Lou, p. 142 Phil6007, p. 154 Clemens Schmillen, p. 218 Jwendsche

Dreamstime:
P. 174-176 Pazemin

Unsplash:
P. 26 yashsavla, p. 28 Max Bovkun, p. 29 amirhanna, p. 36 natamc, p. 38 Moon, p. 44 dariociraulo, p. 45 mostafa meraji, p. 48 evanthewise, p. 55 jannerboy62, p. 56 Marios Gkortsilas, p. 57 Darcey Beau, p. 62 Ismail Merad, p. 68 saj_shafique, p. 76 NajlaCam, p. 102 Muhammad Ahmad, p. 108 Wil Stewart, p. 126 okdara, p. 130 Piotr Chrobot, p. 135 Osama Saleh, p. 144 paul silvan, p. 146 shreyasgupta, p. 147 raldoc, p. 164-167 Riyas Mohammed, p. 170 daviator737, p. 180 bigdodzy, p. 191 nabiloh, p. 200 ihjaaz, p. 208 Maël BALLAND, p. 210 Brooke Lark

Pexels:
P. 30 Christian Konopatzki, p. 68 Miguel Cuenca, p. 96 Walid Ahmad, p. 97 Juliia Abramova, p. 119 Imthiyaz Syed, p. 162 ROMAN ODINTSOV, p. 176 Daniel Ponomarev, p. 188+189 The Lazy Artist Gallery, p. 190 Roderick Salatan, p. 191 Diego F. Parra, p. 194 Oziel Gómez, p. 196 Taryn Elliott, p. 202 Denys Gromov, p. 214+215+216 Taryn Elliott

Printed in Great Britain
by Amazon

53827653R00126